C000007957

A Grim Almanac of
OLD BERKSHIRE

A Grim Almanac of OLD BERKSHIRE

Roger Long

SUTTON PUBLISHING

Sutton Publishing Limited
Phoenix Mill · Thrupp · Stroud
Gloucestershire · GL5 2BU

First published 2004

Copyright © Roger Long, 2004

British Library Cataloguing in Publication Data
A catalogue record for this book is available
from the British Library.
ISBN 0-7509-3511-1

Typeset in 11/13.5 Photina.
Typesetting and origination by
Sutton Publishing Limited.
Printed and bound in England by
J.H. Haynes & Co. Ltd, Sparkford.

*The Grim Almanacs
are from an original idea by Neil R. Storey*

CONTENTS

Introduction 7

January 9

February 23

March 35

April 47

May 59

June 69

July 83

August 95

September 107

October 119

November 131

December 143

Bibliography & Acknowledgements 157

At Newbury a witch perceived to have been walking on water (though she was later found to be floating on a plank), caught the bullets fired by Cromwell's troops and chewed them!

A MOST
Certain, Strange, and true Discovery of a
VVITCH.

Being taken by some of the Parliament Forces, as she was standing on a small planck board and sayling on it over the River of *Newbury*:

Together with the strange and true manner of her death, with the propheticall words and speeches she vsed at the same time.

Sept 28

Printed by John Hammond, 1643.

INTRODUCTION

Book No. 13. Yes, this is the thirteenth book that I have inflicted on the no longer unsuspecting public. Personally I can only shoulder 50 per cent of the blame, as Sutton Publishing approached me with the idea via the lovely Lyn Low of Bookends at Wokingham. They say that an author has made it when publishers approach him (or her) instead of sending a steady stream of sympathetic and photocopied rejection slips. If I have made it the fame is restricted to a couple of counties and the fortune has so far eluded me. I have, as yet, been unable to pack up the day job.

Now to the book: *A Grim Almanac of Old Berkshire*. I looked up grim in my dictionary, incidentally a dictionary that only goes from B to W having shed fifteen pages at either end. 'Grim' – of stern or forbidding aspect, relentless, joyless. Oh dear, I hope my regular readers do not find this book so. I hope I have touched upon the scary, blood-lusting, thrill-seeking, pleasurably frightening side of grim and occasionally the jovial and almost flippant aspect of grim; a sort of Grim(m)s fairy tale. There is, however, one very distinguishable difference between this book and a fairy tale: every one of the 380 reports is absolutely true and taken mostly from newspapers of the time.

Now for the almanac side: I cannot give a dictionary definition of almanac for the reasons stated above, but I think most people know what one is. When I first took on this labour of love I realised it was going to be difficult; murderers, rapists, burglars, suicides, natural catastrophes and even ghosts cannot be relied upon to appear on specific days. For instance you might get three murders on 4 April and then none until 10 July. What was I to do?

Cheat? Nay, too strong a word. Be flexible, that's more like it. Thus 'A' went missing on 1 August, the search party was sent out on 2 and 3 August, the body found on the 4th. 'B' was questioned on the 6th, arrested on the 7th, charged on the 9th, made a local court appearance on the 11th. He appeared at Crown Court on 6 October, was convicted on the 7th, sentenced on the 8th and hanged on the 10th. Therefore the same event gives an author a dozen different opportunities for inclusion. After discovering this flexibility, life became a little easier.

My next problem was to find enough 'grim' facts to fill 365 days (note this isn't an almanac for leap years). After numerous trips to libraries in Newbury, Reading, Slough, Maidenhead, Windsor, Bracknell and Wokingham, it became clear that I would have no trouble filling the book. I began to wonder what to leave out.

Those few readers who have read *Murder in Old Berkshire*, *I'll be Hanged* and *Final Commitment* realise that I have dealt with the vast majority of the county's murders up to 1950. It was impossible to omit these, as it would be impossible to write a 'grim' book without including fifty or so murders. However, I have kept these reports to a minimum and the vast majority of the grim tales here have never been seen in book form before. I hope you enjoy them.

Finally, when I was a kid and watching a Hitchcock film, shaking like a leaf, my old mum would say: 'Don't worry, they are only actors, they'll all be having a cup of tea later.' So, nervous reader, don't worry when you read about burning babies and witches, tortured prisoners, ears being cut off, gossips, and lodgers who decapitated their landladies: it all happened a long time ago. But then I wonder if the Berkshire man who murdered three wives, boiling the last one for lard, resembled the cheerful chappy next door? I leave you with this comforting thought: however bad horrors were in the old days, they are far more prevalent today.

Unfortunately, today's Berkshire, neatly bisected from east to west by the M4, is a strip of land 50 miles long and 10 miles wide – you know, the annoying piece of country between the outskirts of London and welcoming Wiltshire.

'Twas not always so. One day in the early 1970s we awoke to find that Oxfordshire had stolen Abingdon, Faringdon, Wallingford, Wantage and about a dozen villages. We got Slough in return though! (I shall discreetly refrain from mentioning Betjeman.)

At the time of the 'grim' happenings detailed in this book, every site and event was firmly ensconced within the boundaries of the Royal County of Berkshire. I make no apology for this and I cannot be held responsible for the past actions of boundary commissioners. I hope the reader will enjoy reading this book as much as I enjoyed writing it.

Later I intend to go for a stroll on the Berkshire Downs, you know, those hills in the south of Oxfordshire.

Roger Long
Crowthorne, 2004

JANUARY

A gunner from Aldershot could remember nothing since New Year's Eve when he was brought before Wokingham Magistrates Court on 3 January 1937. *(Bob Wyatt)*

1 JANUARY **1863** On New Year's Day 1863 a small party of boys from the newly formed Wellington College at Crowthorne could be seen carrying a long and heavy piece of timber. From Wishmoor Cross along the Devil's Highway and across Broadmoor they laboured until they reached their destination and the applause of their colleagues. The prize, an ancient gibbet, adorned one of the dormitories for several days until it was discovered by Dr Benson, the headmaster. At his insistence the trophy was relocated to the wild and windswept Wishmoor Cross where it ultimately rotted away.

Among the criminals hanged at Wishmoor Cross in the mid-eighteenth century were the Wokingham Blacks. They led a lawless existence. Robbing with impunity, blackmailing and intimidating without fear of the law, they prospered. Terrified of, or related to, the Blacks, the local populace survived a nervy coexistence.

The local gentry, however, grew a little tired of the gang. The Blacks, a nickname gained from their dark attire and blackened faces, were becoming more audacious by the day. Led by William Shorter, the Blacks' actions were swift and awesome. A magistrate, who had killed one of their dogs at Bagshot, returned home to find his house on fire. Sir John Cape, another magistrate who had sentenced a Black to a term of imprisonment, found his new plantation destroyed. The son of a caretaker who had annoyed them was waylaid by four Blacks and beaten to death. A local farmer's son was blasted to death through an open window at Eversley. Thus they maintained their nefarious existence with impunity. The local dignitaries and sheriffs met in secret, many law officers thought to be in the employ of the Blacks were excluded. A very secretive plan was formed.

A trusted man was sent post-haste to London with instructions to contact Sir John Fielding (brother of Henry Fielding, the novelist), Commander-in-Chief of the Bow Street Runners. In the autumn two runners, Chalk and Fowler, especially selected for their rugged countenances and disguised as travelling labourers, arrived at Wokingham fair. The amount of money they spent was conspicuous, and it was but a short time before they were noticed by three young Blacks, who immediately struck up a conversation. Chalk, seemingly the worse for drink, became talkative, much to the annoyance of Fowler. Chalk informed his intent listeners that they were professional witnesses. If a lawyer was a little short of witnesses, to prove a conviction or an alibi, one could be bought and paid for with little trouble from just outside the court. (Incidentally, these men were known as 'strawshoes' because of ears of corn sticking out of their boots showing their availability.) Chalk informed his new friends that some lawyers paid a regular retainer to 'witnesses' and that he would gladly introduce them to such a man at Holborn the following week.

Unbeknown to Shorter and his fellow leaders, the three young Blacks kept a rendezvous with Chalk at a Holborn tavern. As their host bought them a drink they turned to find themselves looking down the barrels of a dozen pistols. Under the persuasion of the Bow Street Runners the Blacks told all, and a complete troop of horse grenadiers was drafted down to the forest. After a pitched battle no fewer than twenty-nine gang members were arrested. William Shorter, however, remained at large with three of his lieutenants. Baptist Nunn of Bigshot Rayles had been intimidated by Shorter into paying him money. Realising that he would be demoralised by the loss of so many men, Nunn informed a trusted sheriff of his intended meeting with Shorter at Crowthorne, the venue for which was a disused hunting lodge. Wary of a trap, Shorter and his men had watched the building for several hours before Nunn arrived, but as they entered the building a dozen runners surrounded them. The four men were taken without a struggle.

The indictments at Reading Court ranged from trespass to murder. Shorter and his three lieutenants were hanged and their bodies hung in chains on various parts of the moor. Shorter himself was displayed prominently at Wishmoor Cross where the three counties and four parishes meet.

1915 Local newspapers reverberated with headlines such as 'Dam Bust'. **2 JANUARY** Mayor Norketts's two-year-old dam at Maidenhead gave way under extreme flood conditions; houses and many acres of farmland were destroyed, but there were no fatalities.

In 1913 Norketts's dam was complete, following many years spent securing both moral and financial support. The dam was said to have been weakened by legal agreements from the start. With the best of intentions, however, the earthworks went up and the unemployed helped trample them down tight. On 15 September 1913 the dam was opened: it was 4ft high, 3ft wide at the top, 15ft wide at the base and 1,000ft long. It was built complete with sluice gates, had cost £300, employed forty-five men in the building work and lasted two years.

1937 A total loss of memory was pleaded by a gunner stationed at Aldershot **3 JANUARY** when he was brought before magistrates at Wokingham. The soldier stated that he had been drinking with friends in town on Christmas Day lunchtime after which he remembered nothing. Sergeant Palmer of Wokingham police said that he arrested the man in Reading Road after the report of three house break-ins in the area. When he was searched at Wokingham police station, the man had secreted about him a notecase, a lady's handbag and a second notecase containing a £5 note. All of these items had been taken from the break-ins. Magistrates decided that because of the gravity of the charges and the vast amount of money concerned the soldier should be sent to the assizes.

1845 This day brought the news of a terrible murder at Salt Hill, Slough. **4 JANUARY** Newspapers reported that Mary Ashley had heard screams coming from the cottage next door, the residence of John Tawell, his common-law wife Sarah Hart and Tawell's two children. As Mrs Ashley approached the house she noticed someone walking quickly away and asked him what was amiss. He ignored her and carried swiftly on. Mary Ashley discovered Sarah Hart in severe pain, and she died before a doctor could be contacted. Dr Champney listened to Mary Ashley's story and her description of the man of Quaker appearance. Realising he could do nothing for Sarah he set out to trace the

A scene from the trial of John Tawell. He was charged with the murder of Sarah Hart at Slough on 4 March 1845. Tawell was the first British criminal to be caught by electric telegraph. (*Author's Collection*)

suspect. Champney knew of Tawell's liking for dressing as a Quaker and it was no surprise to him that Mary Ashley didn't recognise him as he was so seldom at home.

Tawell reached Slough station, took a train west to Windsor, got off and then returned to Slough before going on to London – an obvious attempt to put would-be followers off the scent. Tawell, however, had two pieces of bad luck. Firstly the engine driver noticed his unusual behaviour and secondly the tenacious and resourceful Dr Champney had seen him at Slough station and requested the staff to use the new electric telegraph to contact London police. Sergeant Williams followed Tawell from Bishops Road terminus to a nearby Quaker lodging house. Thinking Tawell to be safe for the night, he retired.

Police raided the lodgings at 7 a.m. but Tawell had already absconded. He was later arrested at the Jerusalem coffee shop known to be a favourite haunt of his. Tawell was tried before Judge Baron Parke in March 1845. There was no shortage of drama: Sarah Hart's mother fainted while giving evidence, and Fitzroy Kelly, Tawell's attorney, brought forth billows of laughter by stating that the prussic acid found in the victim's stomach could have been caused by eating too many apples. A London chemist deposed that

Tawell had bought prussic acid from him the day before the murder and so a farcical alibi was torn to shreds by the prosecution, thereby setting the seal on Tawell's case.

Tawell, showing a misguided confidence, had ordered dinner at the White Hart at Aylesbury. The meal was never eaten. Tawell was convicted, sentenced and hanged, his place in criminal history ensured by being the first murderer entrapped by the new-fangled electric telegraph.

5 JANUARY

1883 At Maidenhead petty sessions a woman, who gave the name of Louise Hedges, was charged with being drunk and disorderly. PC Varney found the prisoner sitting on a water trough singing and carried her to the police cells. She was sentenced to be taken to the edge of town and sent on her way. Also on this day Jake Sexton was convicted of keeping a ferocious dog. The dog attacked neighbour James Hooper. Sexton was fined *3s 6d* and sentenced to ten days in default. The dog was sentenced to death.

6 JANUARY

1776 Twelve prisoners broke out from Reading gaol. On Monday 8 January the *Reading Mercury* and *Oxford Gazette* printed a report of 7 January:

Yesterday morning, between the hours of one and two, 12 prisoners confined in our county gaol for different felonies found means, by the help of a saw, to get into a loft over a cell in which they were usually secured. From this place they contrived a method of getting on to the roof, part of which they untiled and affected an escape by the assistance of a rope. Three of them have since been taken and brought back to their old lodgings and the strictest search is making after the rest.

Nine descriptions then follow and the piece ends with a reward: 'Any person apprehending any of the above felons, shall receive a reward of two guineas for each so apprehending to be paid by me John Hill Gadler'.

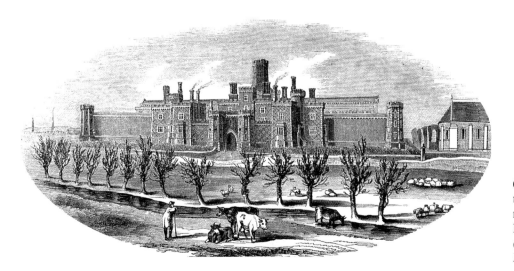

On 6 January 1776 twelve prisoners made an escape from Reading Gaol. *(Berkshire County Library)*

7 JANUARY **1883** *Windsor Borough Epiphany Sessions.* Thomas Edes and William Smith were charged with knowingly possessing two counterfeit shillings. Ann Carroll, common-law wife of Smith, was charged with uttering (putting into circulation) one of the said coins. The case lasted nearly two days and involved over thirty witnesses, including high-ranking officers from Her Majesty's mint and specialised weights and measures personnel. Numerous shopkeepers and police officers were also involved. Smith and Edes were found guilty and sentenced to one year's imprisonment with hard labour. Ann Carroll was also found guilty and sentenced to a year in gaol.

8 JANUARY **1886** Richard Dadd, a very talented artist from a middle-class family, died at Broadmoor Hospital, Crowthorne. In his early twenties he became a member of 'The Clique', mixing with such company as Augustus Egg, William Powell Frith and John Phillip. In 1843 Dadd returned from the Grand Tour and it was noticed by his family and friends that he was mentally unbalanced. He would lock himself in his room and paint pictures of friends with deep gashes across their throats. Dadd's physician, Dr Alexander Sutherland of St Luke's Asylum, advised that Dadd should be confined. Unconvinced, Dadd's father, Robert, took his son on a trip to Cobham in Kent where they took lodgings at The Ship. During a walk by a chalk pit, called Paddock Hole, Richard Dadd committed a frenzied attack on his father with a knife and razor, leaving the poor fellow dead.

Richard Dadd, the artistic genius who murdered his father at Cobham, Kent, died on 8 January 1886 in Broadmoor. The murder took place on 27 August 1843 and the body was later found in a chalk pit which was renamed Dadd's Hole. (*Author's Collection*)

Richard Dadd fled across to France and down to Paris. He might have stayed at liberty a lot longer had he not attempted to cut the throat of a fellow passenger on a stagecoach near Fontainebleau. As a result Dadd was taken into custody in France, extradited to England, taken before Rochester's magistrates and re-manded to the assizes at Maidstone. There he was found unfit to plead and taken to Bedlam Hospital at Southwark. At Bedlam he was permitted to paint and turned out some of his finest works. Later he was transferred to Broadmoor Asylum where he died in 1886.

Also on this day at Windsor Court, Henry Fellows was brought up and indicted with his fifty-first drunk and disorderly charge. Sentence: seven days' hard labour.

The unfortunate William Diggle lived at Broadmoor until his death. *(Stewart Evans)*

1883 At the assizes held at Abingdon, William Henry Bristow (aged eighteen) Samuel Herbert (aged seventeen) and Francis Sanders were put on trial accused of attacking John Barker at New Wood. Two prisoners were accused of stealing a pocket watch and 11s. All three prisoners brought forth a host of witnesses placing them elsewhere at the time of the assault. Verdict: not guilty.

9 JANUARY

1645 The execution of William Laud, Archbishop of Canterbury. Laud was born in Broad Street, Reading, in 1573. He was short and nicknamed 'Little Vermin'. His father and mother were born in Wokingham. His uncle Sir William Webbe was Lord Mayor of London. Laud was educated at Reading Free Borough School and became a fellow of St John's, Oxford. In 1626 he became Bishop of Bath and Wells, Privy Councillor in 1627, Bishop of London in 1628, Master of the Ecclesiastical Situation in 1629 and Archbishop of Canterbury in 1633. Laud was Charles I's right-hand man from 1629 to 1640, a period known as 'The Eleven Years of Tyranny'. This enabled him to be a benefactor to Reading and successfully order its charter. Laud made many enemies and was finally thrown into the Tower by Parliament. In 1645 he was beheaded at Tower Hill.

10 JANUARY

1831 Of all those arrested, charged and convicted after the 1830–1 farm riots only one man in the county of Berkshire was actually hanged. Many were sentenced to death but were finally reprieved and transported for life: England needed strong workers in the Colonies. At noon on 11 January 1831 William Winterbourne climbed the scaffold alone. He knelt briefly in prayer and then, without a word to the small silent crowd, took the drop.

11 JANUARY

1951 William Diggle (aged twenty-six) of Bury, Lancashire, took the Broadmoor dive to death. He had gained access to an outer door while cleaning and eventually found his way to the roof. After waiting ten minutes he made a swallow-dive. At the Coroner's Court death was attributed to haemorrhaging, caused by a skull fracture.

12 JANUARY

13 JANUARY   **1787** John Johnson of Coleport, London, was not expected to live after being beaten in a bare-knuckle fight staged at Wokingham. Johnson fell unconscious after a two-hour boxing match with a man named Ward from Bristol.

14 JANUARY   **1887** Michael Kelly, an extremely dangerous offender, escaped from Broadmoor in an unusual way. While helping a painter outside the walls, Kelly, a native of Boston, Massachusetts, pointed in the direction of a small copse and shouted, 'Look at all those rabbits'. The painter looked away and when he looked back Kelly was running at a great pace some 50yds in the distance. The painter didn't know whether to give chase or sound the alarm. As Kelly was 6ft 4in tall and of an extremely violent nature the painter decided on the latter course. Kelly was never caught, but in 1910 he returned to Broadmoor Asylum. He was a very poor old man and wanted to live the rest of his life secure in Broadmoor. Several retired warders were summoned to verify that the old man's claim to a place at the asylum was genuine; he was identified and permitted to remain.

15 JANUARY   **1898** Richard A. Prince (born Richard Miller Archer) was committed to Broadmoor. Prince, a talentless and poverty-stricken actor, had knifed to death William Terris, a very talented and wealthy actor, outside London's Adelphi Theatre. The motive would seem to have been jealousy. Prince had a chip on his shoulder against Terris, believing he had caused him to be sacked on a previous occasion. On the contrary, Terris had gone out of his way to find Prince walk-on parts (he was capable of little else) and had helped Prince financially on numerous occasions. Doctors and police were soon on the scene, but nothing could save Terris. Prince, who offered no resistance, was apprehended by a man named Greaves who was a long-standing friend and companion of Terris. The Adelphi, where Terris was appearing with Jesse Milward, was closed for a week. On 13 January 1898 Prince pleaded not guilty at the Old Bailey. The poor would-be actor finally had his large audience, but the trial only lasted one day. Prince was found to be guilty but insane, and was soon despatched to Broadmoor.

16 JANUARY   **1766** This was the day of the first Newbury bread riots. A vast number of the poor attacked stallholders at Newbury market. Stalls were overturned and carts burnt. To quiet the mob, bakers reduced their prices by *2d*. Unpacified, the mob marched to Shaw Mill where machinery was smashed and flour dumped in the river. Over the months things worsened: other mills were attacked and a mill-owner killed. Finally troops were called in, order was restored and many marchers were transported.

1828 A gang of no fewer than a dozen young poachers entered the grounds of Crutchley Park, Sunninghill. Splitting into groups of three the men were successful, jubilant and noisy; loud enough, it seems, to attract the attention of head keeper Mansell, who gave chase, blowing his whistle for assistance. Weighed down as the poachers were with firearms and ill-gotten gains, the head keeper was soon within striking distance of them. One man turned and blasted Mansell in the chest; he fell, terribly wounded. Thinking him dead they dragged his body into the undergrowth.

At this point they were approached by Robert Glasspool, the assistant keeper. Summoned by his governor's whistle he had witnessed the actions from afar. Although outnumbered, he was determined to hold on to at least one of the poachers, but he was beaten to the ground and kicked senseless by his adversaries. The three young thugs took to their heels, but not before they had robbed Glasspool of a particularly fine set of new boots.

The keepers were found in a horrendous condition; Mansell survived but was crippled for life. No stone was left unturned as a large troop of constables from four counties and aided by dragoons questioned every known poacher in the area. By the end of February nine men were in custody. Six received lengthy prison sentences for trespass and poaching. Three young men, Henry Burnett (aged twenty-two) of Hounslow, Thomas Field (aged twenty-one) of Egham and Samuel White (aged twenty-one) of Englefield Green, were accused of shooting Mansell, knocking Glasspool to the ground and stealing his boots. The trial was brief and the verdict a foregone conclusion. On 22 March 1828 a vast crowd watched the hangings. The *Reading Mercury* gave a graphic description that ended with: 'Samuel White's rope slipped causing him protracted suffering for several minutes, Burnett died instantly and Field without much pain.'

1891 The Warren Farm tragedy occurred at Wash Common near Newbury. It was a freezing cold night when Superintendent George Bennett arrived at the farm. He was greeted by a demented man and shown two still bodies. The bodies were those of Sydney Heath, who had apparently been shot while playing the piano, and Annie Marie Chamberlain, his sister. She had been shot in the back as she headed for the front door. Sydney at the piano had literally had his brains blown out; they were scattered across the keyboard of the piano and a large part of his skull was in the corner of the room.

The demented man was John Chamberlain, husband of Annie Marie and owner of Warren Farm. An account of the tragedy supplied by Chamberlain was outlined as follows: John had asked Annie to ask her brother to join them that evening. John had made a will and as Annie and Sydney were joint executors, he wanted to discuss some minor details with them. On arrival Sydney, an accomplished pianist, left the others in the kitchen while he amused himself on the piano in the sitting room. After a few minutes Annie stated that she wanted to spend some time with her brother to discuss some matters appertaining to the will. John agreed. Several minutes later John heard the shotgun blast. He rushed in to find his brother-in-law blasted at the piano and his wife holding his shotgun with her finger on the trigger. Fearing that Annie might let loose the other barrel he grappled with her, and this resulted in the fatal wound in his wife's back.

It was John Chamberlain's contention that Annie had intended to kill herself, and a suicide note of sorts was discovered. At the Coroner's Court much was made of Annie's being mentally unbalanced and even more of how she had come to be shot in the back. After much deliberation the jury returned with the verdict of accidental shooting by her husband while she was attempting suicide. They concluded that Sydney Heath was shot by his sister during her temporary derangement. Over the following days there was intense press speculation about John Chamberlain. It was discovered that he had been adopted by the Chamberlains and had been born Moses Belcher Whitehorn. He had already inherited from a previous death and would benefit from Annie's, having recently taken out a massive life insurance on his wife. Makes you wonder, doesn't it?

1939 PC Selwood received a call at Reading's Eldon Road police station at 10.45. The call came from a local police call-box. Selwood listened intently as a man's shaky voice stated: 'Go to 44 Rodway Road – I've lost

PC Selwood answered the telephone at Eldon Road police station to frightened murderer Sydney Pricket. 'Go to 44 Rodway Road', the scared voice said, 'I've lost my head.' *(Berkshire County Library)*

my head'. Asked to elucidate the caller reiterated: 'Just go to 44 Rodway Road', then replaced the receiver. PC Selwood communicated through another police box to PC Trotman of the CID. Trotman in turn rushed to the original box where he found a man who looked ill and white and was shaking uncontrollably. 'I've done her in. Please get me a solicitor. I know I shall be hung,' gasped the shaking man between sobs.

Later Detective Inspector Knight forced his way into 44 Rodway Road, Tilehurst, the home of Mr and Mrs Sydney Pricket. There he found Mrs Edith Pricket lying on a bed. There were pressure marks around her throat and blood on the pillow. She had been dead for some hours. The body was later identified by PC Timms, the unfortunate woman's brother. A post-mortem examination proved that death had been caused by asphyxia.

On 16 May 1939 at Reading Assizes Sydney Pricket was charged with the murder of his wife Edith Pricket. He pleaded guilty but insane. Evidence was given as to Pricket's long history of mental illness. Convicted, he was despatched to Broadmoor Asylum.

17 JANUARY

1872   On this day Broadmoor was the destination of Christiana Edmunds, the notorious Brighton chocolate poisoner. Edmunds was convicted at the Old Bailey of the murder of a young lad, Sydney Albert Barker, and the attempted murder of Mrs Beard, wife of Dr Beard, a Brighton GP. Edmunds had an insatiable infatuation for Dr Beard and found his wife an inconvenience. She therefore sent poisoned chocolates to various residents of Brighton in an attempt to cover up the murder of Mrs Beard. Christiana Edmunds died in Broadmoor in 1907 and was buried in the institution's graveyard.

18 JANUARY

1707   This is said to be the day when Frances Kendrick, a beauty from the famous Reading family, dressed herself as a man and picked a quarrel with a young lawyer named Benjamin Child. A duel was arranged at Calcot Woods. With weapons drawn and seconds at the ready, Frances Kendrick threw down her cloak and mask with the alleged lines:

> It was I that did invite you,
> You shall wed me or I shall fight you.

Child chose the former and they married at Wargrave on 28 May 1707.

19 JANUARY

1915   At Burnham petty sessions William Goom was charged with stealing five trusses of hay, the property of George Edward Dodds. Arthur Joseph Woodley was charged with receiving the same, knowing it to be stolen. As the hay was valued at 12s 6d the case was considered serious enough to go to Reading Assizes.

20 JANUARY

1943   Reginald 'Smiler' Buckfield arrived at Broadmoor Asylum. Smiler had been convicted of the murder of Ellen Ann Symes on 9 October 1942 in Strood, Kent. The unique thing about Buckfield was that while waiting to be charged he wrote a forty-page work of 'fiction', casting himself as a private investigator and Mr X as the villain who slaughtered the young damsel – a thinly disguised version of Ellen Ann Symes. It obviously did no good as Smiler was convicted. He spent many cheerful years at the asylum where he got involved in many and varied activities, not the least of which was being found in very suspicious circumstances with a female warden after lights out.

'Smiler' Buckfield was convicted of murdering Ellen Ann Symes on Friday 9 October at Brompton Farm Road, Strood, Kent. *(Stewart Evans)*

21 JANUARY   **1802**   A Coroner's Court sitting at Maidenhead brought a verdict of accidental death in the case of John Quelch, aged thirty, who died of gunshot wounds while helping his master to 'ramrod home'. The shot took off two of the unfortunate man's fingers before entering his bowel. All present gave sympathy to Quelch's young wife who was about to give birth.

22 JANUARY   **1930**   An inquest was set up concerning the mummified remains of a newborn baby found in the belfry of Thatcham church. Workers maintaining the belfry found the body in a small coffin beside an air vent. The foreman deposed that he had opened a small box and was shocked to find the tiny remains inside wrapped in brown paper. A pathologist suggested that the baby may have been strangled and a local undertaker estimated that the makeshift coffin was forty-five to fifty years old. The jury brought an open verdict.

Thatcham church, where the mummified remains of a newborn baby were found during alterations to the tower. *(Brenda Allaway)*

In 1879 the River Thames, near the ferry at Wargrave, was the scene of a fatal skating accident. The ferrymaster's daughter, ten-year-old Mary Anne Thomas, was drowned. *(Brenda Allaway)*

1870   At Sandhurst, the four-year-old daughter of the head laundress at Wellington College died when her dress caught fire. A neighbour, John Hilton, gave brave assistance by wrapping the girl in his jacket, but unfortunately to no avail.

23 JANUARY

1877   On this day strangers were seen in the Duke's Head and Rose and Crown at Sandhurst. Rumour suggested that they were plainclothes police officers on the lookout for Charlie Peace. Charlie was a brutal murderer who had escaped from police custody. He was thought to frequent the area.

24 JANUARY

1879   January 1879 was the middle of a very harsh winter. At Wargrave, Colonel Markham of Shiplake House had set out with his teenage daughter to go skating on the Thames. Tiring of the sport the colonel hailed the ferry to carry them across the icy water. On the journey the boat was struck by floating ice and capsized. All four occupants (the ferryman was accompanied by his small daughter) were thrown into the freezing water and swept upstream. The colonel and ferryman succeeded in reaching the bank; Miss Markham was pulled to the side near the George and Dragon thanks to the courageous act of two local men, Fisher and Wyatt; but the ten-year-old daughter of Essex Thomas (the ferryman) was unfortunately lost. At the time there was much made of the Markham's unfortunate accident in many local newspapers. The class system being as it was, the ferryman's daughter was only mentioned as an afterthought. It was only quite recently, through the diligence of a local writer, that she was identified as Mary Anne Thomas. Incidentally, there have long been stories of a water ghost near the George and Dragon. A genderless sprite, nicknamed Benji, is said to lure people to their death in the water.

25 JANUARY

1887   At Ascot there was an all-out alert as a man resembling Kelly, the Broadmoor escapee, was sighted at Swinley Woods near Ascot (see the 14th). The man turned out to be a harmless tramp.

26 JANUARY

27 JANUARY   **1877** A horrendous accident occurred at Wellington College. The house of William Barnes, a butler at the college, collapsed killing his infant daughter Ada. At the ensuing inquest at the Waterloo Hotel reactions naturally ran high and there were many emotive outbursts. Several experts brought in by the family's solicitors all agreed that improper and deficient bricks had been used in the building of the house.

Charlie Peace, the 'Devil Man', a master of disguises and amazing escapes. It was thought that the double murderer was once in hiding at Sandhurst. *(Stuart Evans)*

28 JANUARY   **1887** Strangers were seen and thought to be undercover detectives. The men called at the Spotted Cow, the Who'd A Tho't It and the Pig and Whistle at St Sebastian's near Wokingham. It was assumed they were looking for Charlie Peace. Charlie has become a local legend. Many imagine him to be a romantic highwaymen, but nothing could be further from the truth. Charlie Peace was thief and a double (possibly triple) murderer. He finally met his maker at the end of a rope at Armley Prison, Leeds. Charlie's main stamping grounds were Manchester, Leeds and Blackheath. It has never been proved that he even visited the area.

29 JANUARY   **1839** Dr Thomas Peacock of Thames Street hanged himself at Sonning. This was the third of three suicides within the week. Sara Tagg of Sonning Eye drowned in the lock and Mrs Silver threw herself into a pond at nearby Woodley.

30 JANUARY   **1877** This day brought the outcome of the case of Ada Barnes, daughter of the Wellington College butler (see the 27th). The building firm from Sandhurst was found guilty of using inferior materials and was fined £1,000. This crippled the company and put it out of business.

31 JANUARY   **1887** The last day of the month yielded yet another sighting of Broadmoor escapee Michael Kelly, this time at Windsor, and once again it was totally unfounded. It was later proved that by this time Kelly had already sailed for Boston.

FEBRUARY

In 1912 Eton schoolboys ran to the local police station
to report the murder of Anne (Nancy) Saunders. *(Author's Collection)*

1 FEBRUARY   **1787** The body of William Hillimore was discovered on a lonely footpath across Padworth Common. Hillimore had been going to work for 6 a.m. He had left his house at Upton Nervet and was walking the 3 miles to his place of employment. Medical evidence at the coroner's inquest suggested that he had been struck from behind by a heavy instrument. Felled to the ground, Hillimore had sustained further horrendous injuries, probably from the boots of his assailants. The motive for the crime was thought to be the elderly man's prized silver watch. The cowardly assailants had ripped it from his waistcoat and made off, leaving Hillimore to die of his horrific wounds (see the 21st).

2 FEBRUARY   **1940** On this day the ghost of an elderly lady was first witnessed at Shoppenhanger's Manor Restaurant at Maidenhead. Although she has been sighted several times since and is believed to be an elderly waitress, the spirit would seem to pre-date the old building's transformation from a manor house. There would also seem to be a second spirit, a tall gentlemen dressed in grey. This eerie character would seem to value punctuality as he always appears at 2 a.m. This friendly spook is thought to be an old servant who died falling down a staircase. Whether this fatal experience happened at 2 a.m. is a matter of speculation.

3 FEBRUARY   **1831** At Reading County Court the High Sheriff reported on the special courts set up to deal with riots and machinery breaking. He reported that in the last three months 138 people had been arrested and 23 had been sentenced to death. One, William Winterbourne, had been hanged and the remaining 22 transported for life. Twelve had been transported for 14 years, 11 transported for 7 years, 7 had been imprisoned for 18 months, 13 for 12 months, 1 for 9 months, 4 for 6 months, 4 for 4 months and 1 for 3 months. The remainder had been acquitted or the charges had been dropped.

4 FEBRUARY   **1913** On this date Eric Sedgwick had the unenviable distinction of being the last man to be hanged at Reading gaol. At 4.30 p.m. on a freezing November day in 1912, the brooding academic quiet of Eton College was split asunder by the scream of 'Murder! Murder! 'Orrible bloody murder'. The scream came from Annie Saunders, a servant at Cotton Hall House. Annie was inconsolable. 'Fetch the police, Nancy's dead, Eric's murdered her', was her cry. As a master and several boys accompanied Annie down Eton Wick Road to the police station, several masters (one carrying a heavy walking stick) and a host of boys headed for Cotton Hall House. There they found Mrs Booker, the housemaster's wife, blocking the door. 'In there,' she said. 'Be very careful.'

On entering, two masters found the motionless body of Anne (Nancy) Davis. She lay across a chair, bleeding profusely, a long stiletto-type dagger protruded from her breast. In a window alcove stood a weeping, shaking young man, Eric Sedgwick. 'That's my Nancy,' he wept. 'I have killed her.' Sedgwick was charged at Slough Magistrates Court and was remanded to Aylesbury quarter sessions on 20 January.

A brief précis of Edith Armstrong's evidence would seem to cover the sad story. Edith was a maid who shared a room with the deceased. She deposed that Sedgwick and Nancy had endured a very disturbed relationship recently; they had split up but Sedgwick refused to accept this. Sedgwick was trying to resume their relationship but Nancy was having none of it. On 24 November Sedgwick attracted the girl's attention by knocking on the window of Cotton Hall. Nancy pleaded with Edith to tell him to go away. However, Sedgwick made such a rumpus that they were scared Mrs Booker would hear, so they let him in. Edith then got a message to take some mustard upstairs to Mrs Booker. On her return she heard a scream and rushed in to find Nancy dying and Sedgwick holding her to his chest and crying.

Eric Sedgwick was found guilty and sentenced to hang on 4 February. He neither expected nor desired a reprieve and walked manfully to his death at Reading gaol. As the notice of his demise was placed upon the gates a small crowd looked on. According to the *Berkshire Chronicle*: 'they had gratified their morbid curiosity.'

1926 The poltergeist trouble at the old forge at Finchampstead began on this day but had started to settle down by August. The haunting was ferocious, terrifying and witnessed by many. Firstly a bath full of tins and nails was turned over, followed swiftly by chairs doing somersaults, tables moving across the floor and pictures flying from their hooks. Chests were upturned, as were perambulators and bicycles. Bricks flew from solid walls, were replaced and then flew out once more. Bedclothes were ripped from beds, writing appeared on exercise books, doors and walls. The word 'GO' appeared on the ceiling of the bedroom where the whole family slept for safety. A pie was removed from a plate and later found in a coal shed. A tin tray flew across the room and a passing cyclist was nearly decapitated by a fireguard. Most spectacular of all was a 10ft carpenter's bench that took three men to lift – it upended itself while the family slept. The whole place attracted much attention from radio and the national papers. The *Daily Mail* did a series on it until August when the activity subsided. Finally, a police officer, detailed to watch the forge, took a down-to-earth view and warned the family of wasting police time. As he rode away a house-brick struck him on the shoulder.

5 February

1886 An epileptic boy (aged eleven) was charged with setting fire to a barn of hay. He was sentenced as a dangerous lunatic and sent to Broadmoor. Billy Giles spent the next sixty-five years in the asylum and was looked upon more as a member of staff than an inmate. Although given the chance to leave on several occasions, Billy preferred to stay.

6 February

1906 A tragedy occurred at the tiny Broadmoor School. A small girl named McUan was tidying up near the grate when her dress caught fire. Two teachers rolled her in a rug and then rushed her up the hill to the institution where two doctors attended her. Later she was taken to Reading Hospital where she was expected to live but would be terribly scarred for life.

7 February

8 FEBRUARY **1876** At Newbury petty sessions two young local men, Freddie Ward and Hardy Bendall, were charged with poaching on Headley Common. PC Curl deposed that he had cornered the two on the Common but Bendall had grabbed both their weapons and fled. After a struggle the officer apprehended Ward, who stated that he was only out for a walk. At this moment a badly injured pheasant stuck its head out of the prisoner's pocket. Ward and Bendall, who was captured later, were fined 15s with fourteen days' hard labour in default.

9 FEBRUARY **1864** The first male patients began to arrive at Broadmoor. By 31 December there were 309 patients of both sexes.

10 FEBRUARY **1723** The fledgling *Reading Mercury* reported the death of popular and prosperous farmer Jonathan Blagrave. He was extrovert to the extreme, and this was to be his undoing. Having had a financially successful day at the market and also having made a round of the Reading inns, Blagrave was now on his way back to his farm in Upper Caversham. 'Just one more call, the Griffin on Caversham Bridge, would do nicely,' he said to himself. Jonathan Blagrave was soon inside, slapping the backs of farmer friends and boasting of his profits. Unbeknown to Blagrave, a far less cheerful and down on their luck trio of young people sat in the adjoining bar. The two young men and a young lady could easily hear the farmer's boastful merriment. It was 3 a.m. on Sunday morning when Blagrave left the Griffin to make his way up St Peter's Hill and home. The jovial farmer never made it. He was but part-way across the first field when he was attacked by three footpads. His skull was smashed and his money stolen. Defiant to the end the fatally wounded farmer crawled across a field to the Roebuck public house where he later died. The *Mercury* stated several days later that 'three young persons were took up

Boastful Jonathan Blagrave crossed the Thames at Caversham Bridge on 10 February 1723. He was soon to be the victim of a heinous murder. *(Berkshire County Library)*

on suspicion' and finally, 'Ambrose Strange, who killed him, was hanged in chains at Tylers Heath for it.' Nobody seems to know the location of Tylers Heath, but workmen digging in Woodcote Road some 165 years later discovered three bodies – two men and a woman. The bodies had been stretched, which was consistent with being hung in chains.

1876 Newbury petty sessions were in progress. Marshall Lapeard was charged with using abusive language to Mrs Gale, a licensee. Lapeard apologised and paid 5s 6d costs. The mayor also warned Mrs Gale for keeping a disorderly house.

11 FEBRUARY

1796 On the same day, eighty years earlier, fire broke out at a barn in Sonning Eye. The barn belonged to Mr Kent but was rented by James Millard. The whole building was gutted; a wagon, two rollers, a plough and a quantity of wheat were destroyed. Foul play was suspected and a 30 guineas reward offered.

1800 On this day the entire population of Touchen End, near Maidenhead, was shocked by the horrendous murder of Anne Pearman. Anne and her husband Thomas ran a small bakery in the tiny hamlet. At 2 p.m. on that fatal afternoon, Thomas set out with their five-year-old daughter to make some deliveries. At 2.15 p.m. two elderly ladies, approaching Pearman's bakery to purchase some salt, were nearly knocked to the ground by a young man fleeing at great speed. Unable to gain entrance the astonished women heard moaning coming from within; a neighbour was fetched and the lock broken.

12 FEBRUARY

The pretty village of Bray, home of John Hutt, who viciously murderered Anne Pearman of Touchen End. *(Brenda Allaway)*

Inside a young woman lay prostrate, her skull had been smashed with such force that blood splattered the floor and ceiling of her spotless kitchen. Anne was alive but died shortly after. The weapon used was a faggot of wood from outside the shop; a young man had been seen whittling there earlier. The two elderly ladies and various other witnesses described a stocky albino youth, 5ft tall, with an extremely florid complexion and a massive mop of white hair.

Naturally there were very few people of such a description. John Hutt of nearby Bray was suspected immediately. The suspicion was endorsed by the fact that he had left the area soon after the event. John Hutt was picked up heading for Portsmouth. He was found guilty and sentenced on 4 March 1800. In the early nineteenth century there was no appeals system, and Hutt was executed forty-eight hours after conviction. As was usual in those days the judge directed that the corpse be dissected at Reading town hall.

1817 On the same day seventeen years later a reward of £20 was offered for the arrest of Charles Dormer of Wokingham, who was wanted for numerous felonies. He was tall (5ft 7in), had grey eyes and slouched when he walked.

13 FEBRUARY **1817** Father Longuet, Reading's eccentric Roman Catholic priest, was found murdered in Oxford Road. The priest was attacked as he rode his horse back to town after preaching at Wallingford. The poor man's head had been beaten so badly that most of it had gone. In addition to a fractured skull Longuet had received five stab wounds and his money belt had disappeared. An exceptionally large reward of 200 guineas was offered.

14 FEBRUARY **1320** It is thought that Thomas Jarman, landlord of the Ostrich at Colnbrook, was executed for his crimes on this day. Jarman would ply a wealthy traveller with drink until he was quite drunk and then lead the unfortunate traveller

A working model of the contraption at the Ostrich Inn, Colnbrook. The landlord, Thomas Jarman, would pull a lever, tipping his guest into a vat of fat below. (*Author's Collection*)

up to his best room. When the unsuspecting man was deep in slumber Jarman would pull two bolts from the room below. The bed was screwed to the floor and would tip at a 45° angle, depositing the sleeper into a vat of boiling fat below.

Jarman would then take the victim's belongings, sell his horse to the gypsies who were camped on Longmoor and deposit the body in the nearby brook. There are many theories on how he was caught. One is that the body of his last victim, a man named Coln (hence Colnbrook), failed to make it down to the Thames. Another is that his pot boy witnessed the deed and reported him. Yet another is that his prospective victim was attending to the call of nature when he noticed his bed slowly tilting. Whichever, Jarman was hanged for his crimes. Unrepentant on the scaffold he boasted of sixty victims. A truer number, however, is estimated to be nearer fifteen.

1883 At Windsor petty sessions James Cassidy was charged with being drunk, using abusive language and assaulting PC James. The bench was treated to a 15-minute oration on Cassidy's heroic feats in two wars and over a dozen battles. Cassidy stated he was a man of honour, an upright and much respected citizen and had been pushed into the police officer by a member of the crowd. Total balderdash, stated the chairman of the bench, fining Cassidy 10*s* with fourteen days in default.

15 February

1740 John Clark was sentenced to death for robbing the Duke of Marlborough's coach between Reading and Maidenhead of £90 and for twenty-three other highway robberies. He was tried at Leicester Assizes.

16 February

1872 At 2 a.m. on this moonlit Saturday morning the citizens of Lambeth were awakened by three pistol shots. Minutes later police discovered George Merritt, a local brewery worker, lying dead. Dr W.C. Minor was arrested on the spot without the slightest of struggles. Charged with murder Minor, an American by birth, was found to be insane and sent to Broadmoor. There he remained until his release in 1910.

17 February

On 1 March 1879 James Murray was given the task of producing a new English dictionary. He advertised in libraries, newspapers and periodicals, asking for people to forward to him the meanings of obscure words. Many hundreds of people provided thousands of words, but one of the most interesting and prolific was a W.C. Minor. It was many years before the dictionary was complete and at the final publication W.C. Minor was invited to a special celebration. The romantic version of this story is that as Minor had written explaining that he could not attend, so Dr James Murray arranged to meet him at his home. He was surprised and slightly mystified when a coach picked him up at Crowthorne station and took him behind the forbidding walls of Broadmoor. This story is not true. Murray certainly visited Minor at Broadmoor, but he was fully conversant with Minor's situation before his visitation. The full story may be read in Simon Winchester's *The Surgeon of Crowthorne*.

18 FEBRUARY **1835** On this day the *Windsor Gazette* provided its readers with this little gem under the heading 'Strange Bedfellow':

> An old woman, living in Castle Hill, was unspeakably surprised when awakened from a night's rest to find a strange animal lying at her back with its paws about her shoulders. Screaming, she shot out of the bed; the animal leaping to the corner of the room. Struggling to light a candle the lady ran from her front door. When in the street she became a little more composed and remembered the fact that Mr Wombwell had stationed his animals at the pound. Making her way to the pound she contacted Mr Wombwell of Wombwell's Zoo. After checking his stock Wombwell decided that one of his kangaroos was missing. The animal had apparently made its escape up Castle Hill and finding the poor lady's door ajar had decided it was complimentary lodgings for the night.
>
> The kangaroo has now been returned to Mr Wombwell and the good lady has been remunerated for the night's lodgings.

19 FEBRUARY **1742** It was reported that both the Reading stagecoach and another on the Henley to Oxford run were robbed on Maidenhead Thicket by two highwaymen: 'Well mounted, [they] behaved with as much civility as their profession would allow.'

20 FEBRUARY **1883** Mr M.F. Weedon, the Bracknell coroner, reported that he had been called to Broadmoor Asylum five times in one week for inquests into the deaths of patients. All of the patients were recorded as having died of natural causes.

One of the ancient earthworks on Mortimer Common. Abraham Tull and William Hawkins were hanged in chains here in 1787 after being convicted of the most brutal of murders. (*Brenda Allaway*)

1787 Abraham Tull and William Hawkins were found guilty of the murder of William Hillimore at Padworth. They were sentenced to death by Sir Nash Grote, and it was stated that after their execution the bodies would be hung in chains on Mortimer Common. Tull's father, sister and brother watched the executions from a cart. As the ladders pulled away Hawkins died immediately, but Tull endured five minutes of agony.

1805 Mrs Lidderfell, a resident for many years of Windsor Castle and sister to the Bishop of Kildare, died horrendously in her home. She was cooking, in the absence of her servant, and accidentally caught fire and was burnt in the most dreadful manner. Mrs Lidderfell expired at 3 a.m.

1676 George Broome was a farm labourer from East Woodhay. George had a wife Martha, who was devoted to him. He also had a son, Robert, a bright lad of six who idolised his father. Unfortunately George became besotted with Dorothy Newman, a local barmaid who lived over at Inkpen with her two young sons. Dorothy became impatient; Martha must go, otherwise there was no point to this clandestine relationship. She began to flaunt herself to make George jealous. In desperation George devised a plan. Martha brought him hot pasties every day at work, so Dorothy should hide and cudgel Martha to death as she made the trip. George would then report her missing and the crime would no doubt be blamed on some itinerant tramp. The plan was put into action the next day. The unsuspecting Martha was clubbed to death then dumped in a nearby pond. Unfortunately for the couple, Robert had followed his mother and had witnessed the heinous action. Dorothy at once grabbed the boy and held his head under the water until he too was motionless. The two murder-

Combe gibbet, where George Broome and Dorothy Newman met their maker. (*Author's Collection*) ers sped towards their respective homes. Unbeknown to them, however, two other pairs of eyes had also witnessed the scene; Dorothy's two sons had felt something was amiss and reported it to the authorities.

George and Dorothy were arrested. George Broome, a broken man since the death of his son, told all. Convicted at Winchester, the pair were sentenced to hang at Combe, midway between their two villages. The gallows were specially erected and used only once. Combe lay right on the Hampshire/Berkshire border and both counties claimed it. Hants constables were not keen on hanging the couple. Berks constables, less squeamish, elected to do so on the understanding that Combe was from that point forever in Berkshire. The pair were hanged on 22 February 1676.

23 FEBRUARY   **1830**   The first case on the opening day of Reading Lent Assizes was that of George Charlwood of Windsor, who pleaded guilty to breaking into a house at Sunninghill and stealing a looking-glass and two picture frames. The sentence was transportation for life and a month's hard labour until the passage could be booked.

24 FEBRUARY   **1883**   Mr Weedon, the Bracknell coroner, returned to Broadmoor Asylum where three more deaths had occurred. On one occasion Mr Weedon had just opened his door at Easthampstead when he was recalled to Broadmoor.

25 FEBRUARY   **1833**   This was the day that John Carter of Lambourn was hanged in Reading. On 2 February John Carter went to his employer, Mr Spicer, and asked for a raise. The farmer refused, saying that Carter was slack and idle and lucky to be keeping his job. In a morose and vengeful mood Carter returned to a local inn where he had already spent most of the day. At about 9 p.m. Carter called on a colleague, William Winkwood, and borrowed some rags, a large match and some lamp oil. He proceeded to farmer Spicer's barn and torched it. He then returned to the inn, greeting several acquaintances on the way. Shortly after, Carter and a fellow tippler, Henry Rider, strode up the hill to watch the blaze. The barn was soon gutted, with valuable stock and several horses destroyed. The following day Carter was arrested and charged with arson. Also arrested, but later discharged, were Henry Rider and William Winkwood. Carter's trial was brief and virtually academic. With little regret from the populace Carter met his maker at the end of a rope at Reading.

26 FEBRUARY   **1579**   This day saw the conclusion of the Windsor witch trials, a rehearsal both strange and true of heinous and horrible acts committed by Elizabeth Style (alias Rockingham), Mother Duttel, Mother Devell and Mother Margaret. The four notorious witches, apprehended at Windsor and Abingdon, were arraigned, condemned and executed.

27 FEBRUARY   **1825**   In the early afternoon two Eton scholars became involved in a heated argument. Blows were exchanged but the two antagonists were soon

separated by a school captain. Honour, however, was not satisfied. A pugilistic contest was arranged for the following afternoon. Both boys, the Hon. F. Ashley Cooper, aged fifteen, and George Alexander Wood came from two of the county's finest aristocratic families. The engagement commenced at 4 p.m. Wood, being some 6in taller and much the stronger of the two combatants, had twice floored Cooper by round ten. Fortified by brandy poured down their throats by their supporters, the young gentlemen had fought an incredible sixty rounds, when, at well past 6 p.m., Cooper received a blow to the face which pitched him heavily upon his head. He lay there unconscious. His friends carried his inert body to the house of the Revd Knapp where he later died.

On 9 March 1825 George Wood, aged seventeen, and Alexander Wellesley Leith, aged thirteen, were charged at Aylesbury with the unlawful slaying of the Hon. F. Ashley Cooper. Never have so many well-known lawyers appeared in one small courtroom. Mr Justice Gaseler, presiding, requested that the prosecution bring forward their witnesses, of which there were many. However, after a protracted whispering and nodding of knowledgeable heads, none was called and the prosecution decided not to proceed with the case.

Eton College, where two pupils fought with their fists in 1825 until one lay dead. *(Michael Stiles)*

28 FEBRUARY **1908** The body of a man was discovered in the Blackwater at Sandhurst. Despite extensive enquiries and media coverage the identity of the man was never discovered.

Incidentally, some years later a retired local policeman told me that he and his sergeant were instructed to retrieve a body from the Blackwater. It was early evening and both officers were due to play in a local football match. On arrival at the scene, and bearing in mind the lengthy paperwork involved, the sergeant cut a branch and pushed the body to the other side of the river. The corpse was now in Yateley and therefore the responsibility of the Hampshire police instead of the Berkshire Force. The two officers then had time to report to their football match. On arriving for duty the following morning they were surprised to be detailed to the same job. Apparently, overnight, the Hampshire police had pushed the body back.

MARCH

Wantage, where George King searched for lodgings after decapitating his landlady in 1834.
(Author's Collection)

1 MARCH   **1784** 'John Steptoe executed at Reading for sheep stealing.' This is the complete report filed in the *Mercury* on this day.

2 MARCH   **1885** With his second conviction for larceny William Johnson of Arborfield was sentenced to transportation for fourteen years. This is the last record of a Berkshire person being punished in this way.

1882 Also on this day Roderick McClean shot at, but missed, Queen Victoria at Windsor station. He was found not guilty by reason of insanity and sent to Broadmoor. The Queen was outraged and commented: 'Insane he may be, but guilty he certainly was; I saw it with my own eyes.'

3 MARCH   **1834** George King was hanged at Reading for the murder of Ann Pullin, licensee of the White Hart at Wantage. King was a stout and somewhat backward itinerant worker, who was working at nearby Court Hall Farm cutting beans; his only possession other than his white hat was his beanhook. King, who was lodging locally with Ann Pullin, was seen leaving the White Hart at 9.45 p.m. by William Berridge, a fellow licensee of the nearby Blue Boar. King visited the Blue Boar just as Berridge was closing at 10 p.m. Berridge described him as nervous and shaking. He drew some coinage out of his purse and Berridge noticed a bent sixpence. King stayed but a short while and left with a French boy called Marriot, who slept in an attic above a local stable.

On the following day James Pullin, stepson of Ann Pullin, was creeping downstairs hoping not to awaken anybody. It was 5 a.m. and 12-year-old James was off on a fishing expedition. On opening the bar parlour door James noticed a massive pool of blood drenching the carpet. His 40-year-old stepmother's decapitated body lay 4ft away from her head.

It was not long before King was arrested; he was taken by constables while cutting beans at nearby Hanney. He denied all knowledge of the murder, but Berridge and several other witnesses placed him at the right place at the right time. The bent sixpence also helped in his undoing, as did Ann Pullin's purse and a blood-drenched jacket found upon his person.

At the Coroner's Court on 2 September, George King was charged with murder and ordered to be held until Reading Lent Assizes. Still protesting his innocence, King was taken by cart from Wantage to Reading. Midway through the journey the small party stopped at The Bull at Streatley for refreshments. Seeing by chance a portrait of a lady that closely resembled Ann Pullin, King broke down completely, sobbed and screamed that her eyes were following him, begged forgiveness and confessed.

On the morning, 3 March 1834, George King took the drop without uttering a word. Incidentally, Ann Pullin's close relatives had an eye to profit. They charged 1*d* each to a long queue of her former customers to see her laid in state, her head several inches from her body.

4 MARCH   **1824** For many years mothers in north-west Berkshire had a foolproof way of getting their children to come in at night. They would shout: 'Old Danny

Grimshaw will get you.' It was well known that Old Danny Grimshaw grabbed young children and boiled them alive.

Danny Grimshaw the shepherd (in fact aged twenty-two), came home after a long night with no sleep to his pretty wife Anne and baby son Billy.

Anne left Danny brewing tea while she went shopping at Sutton Courtney. Anne had only gone a few yards when there was a terrible scream from the house.

Sutton Courtney church. (*Berkshire County Library*)

Rushing back with a neighbour, Mrs Dew, she found the tiny writhing body of Billy scalded terribly from head to foot. Danny was sitting, head in hands. Dr West, arriving post-haste, found not only external damage but also that the baby's lips, throat and gums had been hideously blistered and burnt. 'Did you pour boiling water down this child's throat?' he demanded of Grimshaw. Danny Grimshaw did not answer but merely strode away, later to be arrested by two constables at the Fish Inn at Sutton Bridge. Ten agonising days later Billy was dead. At his trial Danny Grimshaw stated that he had boiled a basin of water for shaving and had then tripped and accidentally poured it over young Billy. Justice Garrow summed up at great length. He went as far as stating the improbability of guilt. The jury, however, were having none of it. They found the case proven. The papers stated that Justice Garrow was very disconsolate about the verdict as he passed the terrible sentence. Danny

The Fish Inn at Sutton Bridge, where Danny Grimshaw attempted to drown his sorrows after he had scalded his son to death. (*Berkshire County Library*)

Grimshaw, a lamenting and probably innocent man, made a pitiful spectacle as he climbed the scaffold on 4 March 1824.

5 MARCH **1883** On this day a virtual battle took place in Maidenhead. The Blue Ribbon (teetotal) Brigade, complete with flags and drums, marched through the town centre. Near Chapel Arches, the Yellow Army, of the opposite persuasion, fell upon the enemy causing a host of grievous wounds. Many were arrested on minor charges and three, including a landlord, were sent for trial.

6 MARCH **1922** Miss Steel, a young maid to Gertrude Yates, called at her mistress's Fulham flat and found her dead in her bathroom. Gertrude Yates, who lived under the name Olive Young, was a lady of somewhat lax virtue, and had been beaten to death with a rolling pin. Much of her expensive jewellery was missing. Miss Steel stated that she had seen a man leaving. It was Ronald True, one of Miss Yates's regular friends. True was soon arrested and charged, and at his trial he was found guilty. True's family were rich and powerful aristocrats and could buy the

Ronald True was a young man from a good family. He was convicted of slaying prostitute Gertrude Yates, who had been living under the alias of Olive Young. True was sent to Broadmoor, which caused a public outcry. *(Stewart Evans)*

best, and although an appeal was dismissed, Mr Justice McCardie then wrote to Edward Short, the Home Secretary, with a full record of medical evidence from the country's three most qualified experts. All agreed that True was insane at the time of the murder. Ronald True went not to the execution shed but to Broadmoor. This brought a public outcry, which was further inflamed by the fact that at the same time Henry Jackoby, a working-class murderer, had been hanged. True died in Broadmoor in 1950.

1831 John Robinson, a carrier from Steventon, was charged with murdering his wife, Mary. Moses, their son, deposed that as he was unharnessing the horses he heard a violent quarrel between his parents. There was a scream and his mother came out bleeding profusely. Moses had sought the help of Elizabeth May, their next-door neighbour. When Mary's stockings were removed it was discovered that her leg was gushing with blood. She died half an hour later.

At the trial John Kimber, a local blacksmith, said that he had been called to restrain Robinson and was forced to chain him as he was trying hard to commit suicide. At Berkshire Lent Assizes, Robinson asked to be hanged. The judge, however, stated that he was sure a lot of drink had

Wellington College was the scene of a fatal accident in 1881. One pupil was killed when his schoolmates were playing with a gun. Youthful inexperience brought tragic consequences. *(Author's Collection)*

been taken before the incident and sentenced Robinson to six months' imprisonment.

1881 This day brought another tragedy to Wellington College. Three boys, frolicking with a pistol in Wellington's dormitory, accidentally fired it, and the ball went through the eye of one of the young scholars. Although the eye was removed by the college physician and a Harley Street specialist, fetched by stagecoach, it was too late to save the boy. The unfortunate youth was later identified as Harold Mann, son of the famous General Gother Mann.

7 MARCH

1831 At the Maidenhead bench William Stubbles was charged with stealing a tame rabbit from George Keeling of Cookham Dean. Keeling, unable to locate his rabbit, was upset to find its head and skin at the bottom of the garden. He took the remains to Constable Hall. The constable, acting on information received, called at the house of the accused where he found Stubbles's dog munching a cold rabbit. When Stubbles stated that whatever his dog had fetched in, it had come from the Common, Constable Hall replied: 'He made a fine job of skinning it.' Stubbles was remanded to the petty sessions.

8 MARCH

1867 A Boxford youth, George Brind, was accused of indecently assaulting Lettisa Elliot (aged thirteen) as she was returning from school. Magistrates gave Brind the benefit of the doubt when he claimed it was rough horseplay. Verdict: not guilty.

9 MARCH

10 MARCH **1884** Law officers at Maidenhead were berated in the local press for the amount of unsolved break-ins in the affluent village of Cookham. There had been ten burglaries in eight days. The felon was never caught but a travelling knife-grinder was treated with a great deal of suspicion.

11 MARCH **1883** In Maidenhead the Blue Ribbon Brigade, which had not been deterred by recent incidents, held another gathering in the town hall. Captain Mrs Brown brought forward Robert Whall. Whall stated that he had been a drunk since the age of eight; he had lost his business, his wife, his children and his self-respect. He had spent many nights in gaol and had once been arrested in his underpants at Ascot races, having pawned his clothes to back the horses. As the old song goes:

> When you've had a jolly good day at the races,
> Lost your shirt, your collar, your tie and your braces.

12 MARCH **1869** Alice Kaye, a female inmate of Broadmoor, slipped over the lower wall in the middle of the day and was never seen again.

In 1867 Eli Talbot, a carter's apprentice, was accused of running away from his master, Mr Drewitt. Talbot complained that he was regularly physically abused when Drewitt returned after spending the day at the Halfway Inn. (*Brenda Allaway*)

1803   Dennis Daley was led to the gallows at Reading by the Revd Barry.
Daley, an industrious Irishman, had got into debt and forged the name of his
employer on a bill of sale for £10, which he presented to a Reading
shopkeeper. At his conviction the judge stated: 'That for a crime of such
magnitude as this there could be no pardon.' Daley's final words to the crowd
before he was hanged were: 'Good Christians, I beg you to pray for me.'

1867   At Newbury petty sessions Eli Talbot, a country-looking lad, ran away
from a carter named Drewitt. Talbot proclaimed that Drewitt abused him
when drunk, and that Drewitt had spent all day in the Halfway Inn. Talbot
was found guilty and sentenced to one month without pay, and threatened
with the birch next time he absconded.

1916   One Sunday evening the village of Holyport was roused by the sound of
law officers blowing whistles. A German officer was thought to have escaped
from the nearby internment camp. Later the officer, Lieutenant Frier Von-
Groter, was found trapped in a tunnel. Incidentally, there was a pub at
Holyport named the Eagle and when accompanied outside the camp German
prisoners used to salute it (the Eagle being their national emblem). The
authorities were not pleased: the Eagle's board was pulled down and the name
changed to the Belgian Arms.

1923   On this day local papers were of the opinion that a ghost was abroad
near Caesar's Camp. The spirit, ragged and weeping, had been spotted on
several occasions. It was thought to be that of an old miserly miller who, in
the sixteenth century, turned away a starving man only to find him dead on
his doorstep the following morning. After this action a dozen or more
tragedies occurred at the mill until the penniless owner went mad and left to
roam the Broadmoor Forest.

1867   It was announced at Broadmoor that there had been five escapes during
one week. None of the missing inmates was thought to be dangerous.

1820   George Wiggins (aged twenty-two) was hanged at Reading after being
found guilty of cruelly beating and robbing one James Leach on the road at
Thatcham. Wiggins mounted the scaffold with penitence after admitting
eleven highway robberies, eight burglaries and over forty thefts. Not a small
record for one so young.

1883   Lady Florence Dixie reported that she had been attacked and stabbed
near her home, the Fisheries, near Windsor. Wife of Sir Alexander Beaumont
Dixie and sister to the Marquess of Queensbury, Lady Dixie was a
controversial figure. She was an enthusiastic member of the Humanitarian
League, vigorously joining its attack on the Royal Buckhounds when they
were hunting in Windsor. Lady Dixie was also a poet, a war correspondent, a
novelist, an accomplished horsewoman, a swimmer, a rousing platform

speaker and an explorer. She had brought a jaguar and a tiger back from Patagonia.

Lady Dixie stated that she thought her attackers to be Fenians. She was walking with her St Bernard dog, Hubert, in the grounds of the Fisheries when she noticed that two women were following her. They attacked her with knives, proving to be men in female disguise, and left her unconscious. When she awoke she was alone and assumed that her faithful dog had thwarted the attack. Scotland Yard investigated but could find no mud on her dress and the 'knife holes' in her clothes didn't match up with the small cuts on her body. The story of the attack had little credibility but much publicity, so much so that Queen Victoria sent down the worthy John Brown to investigate. Brown found nothing new, but he did catch a chill from which he died shortly after.

20 MARCH

John Brown, the great friend of Queen Victoria, was sent to investigate a reported attack on Lady Florence Dixie in 1883. Was it a genuine attack, or simply accountable to the lady's vivid imagination? Brown failed to discover the truth but he caught a fatal chill. (*Berks, Bucks & Surrey Advertiser/Maidenhead Library*)

1835 John Spicer, a Reading weaver, was hanged in front of a vast crowd of over 6,000 people. Spicer's was not a heinous, brutal or even colourful murder: he had simply had enough henpecking tyranny. The wire snapped, the worm turned and, unthinkingly, he brought down a poker many times on the cranium of his ill-fated spouse.

Realising what he had done in the back of his tiny basket-maker's shop in Reading's Oxford Road, Spicer proceeded to drag the body downstairs, place the head against some flat-irons, loosen the stair-rail and wipe the poker. He then nonchalantly walked into the street. Returning some fifteen minutes later, Spicer inquired of the several waiting customers: 'Where is my wife? Is she not serving you?' Spicer went searching for his wife downstairs.

ATTEMPTED ASSASSINATION OF LADY FLORENCE DIXIE.

Oxford Road, Reading, was the home of the town's 'mild murderer'. John Spicer was the worm that turned. *(Berkshire County Library)*

Customers patiently waiting above then heard him screech: 'My wife! My poor dear wife! Somebody fetch the police.' Police came and were soon very suspicious. There were blood-stains on the carpet between the table and the cellar door. At the coroner's inquest Spicer was indicted for murder. At his trial the most damning evidence came from two forensic experts, both of whom agreed that Mrs Spicer's injuries were inconsistent with her striking her head on flat-irons. Spicer was sentenced to death. The basket-maker had gained his freedom, albeit briefly.

1867 Newbury petty sessions had to deal with a vagrant problem in the town. John Ward, a tramp convicted of stealing bread in Bartholomew Street, was sentenced to twenty-one days' hard labour. Charles Adler, found sleeping rough in Market Square, unreformed after two previous jail terms, was sentenced to a further six months' imprisonment. Charles Wilson, claiming he had sold his daughter's clothes, stated he had friends in Marlborough and was sent on his way. Another dozen or so cases followed. 21 MARCH

1735 The Greyhound coaching inn at Maidenhead was burnt to the ground. Of thirty-three standing beds only three remained. Only three featherbeds and 22 MARCH one pewter pot survived the blaze. All plates, money and books were lost. The fire was thought to have started in a maid's room. The owners, Mr and Mrs Freeman, were away in London at the time. A police officer stated that all the servants were being held in custody.

1844 Thomas Jennings of Oxford Road, Reading, had the dubious distinction of being the first person to hang at Reading's new gaol. In December 1843 Jennings's four-year-old son Eleazer was taken violently ill. A few days later he died. Obviously this was not unusual at a time when infant mortality rates were high and nearly 60 per cent of children didn't reach puberty.

However, suspicion was aroused when Jennings's seven-year-old daughter was also taken ill. An inquiring doctor thought the symptoms to be consistent with arsenic poisoning. The young girl stated that when her father fed the children he placed a saucer of white powder near her plate. Jennings had informed her that it was salt and she had dunked her food in it. After being told that this habit coincided with the young girl's illness and that it had been practised shortly before Eleazer died, the doctor contacted the police. Things moved swiftly; Jennings was arrested, his son's tiny cadaver was exhumed and traces of arsenic were found in the stomach.

Jennings was sentenced to hang. As he climbed the platform he was screamed at and abused by 10,000 people, the majority of whom were women. He was hanged at 10 a.m. still proclaiming his innocence.

The monument to Henry West, who was blown to his death by a freak whirlwind in 1839. *(Brenda Allaway)*

1800 The only man in Berkshire ever to receive the death penalty for bestiality was hanged on this day. Thomas Cox (aged twenty) from Tilehurst was sentenced to death at Reading on 18 March. The facts of the case, are not known, but as bestiality was common in all country areas one can only assume that Cox's actions had offended somebody of importance. The *Reading Mercury* stated that Cox walked to his death with dignity.

1866 It was reported on the same day that Dr Meyer, the superintendent of Broadmoor, was improving. Local newspapers had described how a patient using a flint wrapped in a handkerchief had attacked Dr Meyer while he was attending Holy Communion in the asylum's chapel.

1839 Henry West, a glazier working on the roof of Reading station, was swept to his death when a freak whirlwind removed several tons of the new structure. There is a memorial plaque dedicated to him in St Lawrence's churchyard, Reading.

1815 Probably one of the saddest executions took place on this day in 1815. John Newbank had been convicted and sentenced earlier that month for defrauding John Gammay of Wallingford by offering him a forged £1 note. Two young ladies, thought to be Newbank's daughters, wept openly and a whole host of silent people watched Newbank take the drop. A diarist writing at the time stated that Governor Eastaff was so moved that he had to hold on to the rails to steady himself.

1814 Charles White, horse stealer, took the drop at Reading. White had been found guilty on two charges of stealing horses in the town. The papers described White as notorious in six counties and head of a vast family of thieves, robbers, burglars and miscreants of every conceivable persuasion.

In 1812 White's family had been somewhat depleted at Aylesbury, when no fewer than four of his sons mounted the gallows. A plan to escape the previous night after murdering the prison chaplain had to be abandoned at the eleventh hour. White seemed in a jovial mood (possibly down to strong ale) as he took a front-row seat at the executions. As each son took the drop he boasted about each one's expertise in horse stealing.

Like his sons, White had 'lived and died by the sword'. He took his punishment without 'admission of guilt or contrition of soul'.

1867 It was obvious in Newbury that petty crime would not be tolerated. On this day at Newbury petty sessions, George Trayhorn, a man of previous good character, was sentenced to six weeks' imprisonment. Trayhorn's crime: stealing a rod and line, value *2s.*

1799 To prove that life was no easier in the Services, an unnamed soldier was drummed out of his regiment for stealing wine. The unfortunate man was also to receive 450 lashes at Windsor and Eton.

29 MARCH **1802** On this day Edward Painter was executed at Reading gaol for the theft of two heifers from Mortimer fair. Painter met his maker with penitence and contrition, leaving a wife and ten sorrowing children. How Painter managed to perpetrate this crime let alone conceal his ill-gotten gains is a mystery. One can only imagine that the poor man was driven by desperation to feed his brood.

30 MARCH **1802** The *Reading Mercury* reported that John Ryan was hanged at the town gaol for the murder of Henry Frewin of Burchetts Green. Frustratingly, this was the only observation local papers made on the case.

31 MARCH **1916** Before magistrates at Maidenhead, Lieutenant Frier Von-Groter was sentenced to nine months' imprisonment at Chelmsford. He had been caught attempting to escape from the German internment camp at Holyport (see the 15th). A rather verbose Adjutant Armstrong went into great detail, describing how he courageously pulled Lieutenant Frier Von-Groter back down the tunnel by his boots.

APRIL

Constable Flower and the local blacksmith broke four staves
before subduing the railway rioters outside the Bull at Sonning
on 20 April 1838. *(Brenda Allaway)*

The Dog and Duck at Elmbrook, where an inquest was held into the tragic death of four-year-old Thomas Brooker in 1852. *(Brenda Allaway)*

1 APRIL 1852 On this day a very sad inquest was held at the Dog and Duck, Elmbrook, near Wokingham. Coroner Clarke Esq examined the tiny cadaver of four-year-old Thomas Brooker. The boy had burned to death at his cottage in the village. Mrs Brooker said that she had left the lad with several older children while she called on a neighbour. Apparently Thomas's clothes had caught fire. A verdict of accidental death was pronounced. In closing, Coroner Clarke gave thanks to Mr Burr of Wokingham for his courageous action in bursting into the cottage to extinguish the fire.

2 APRIL 1854 Louisa Parsons, a young serving maid aged twenty-two, attended a party at Playhatch near Caversham. It was a lively party until part-way through the proceedings when Louisa developed bad stomach cramps. She was taken home but her condition worsened. Louisa's parents were country folk and the doctor called was irritated by having to work with Granny Patin – a self-appointed cure-all from Mapledurham. The following morning Louisa Parsons died. There is no record of an autopsy being carried out. Louisa's parents ranted that she had been poisoned at the party. The police were called but no one was charged. It was extremely debatable if any crime had taken place. Louisa's parents were adamant and consulted Granny Patin as to the wording on the tombstone:

> Sacred to the memory of Louisa
> daughter of George and Mary Parsons
> died April 1854 aged 22 years
> all you young people, as you pass by
> pray on my grave, now cast an eye
> beware false lovers and their friends
> I died from poison you may depend

Local people objected to the word poison and the Parsons were ostracised. The situation deteriorated badly when Dr Hawtry became rector of Mapledurham. He found the words distasteful, even more so when he discovered they were composed by a witch. An uneasy compromise followed when some of the more offensive words were covered over.

1867 At Windsor George Binfield of Clewer was charged, together with a man named Ward (yet to be taken in custody), with stealing a bundle of withy rods, the property of James Boyce of Clewer Green. He was committed to Reading gaol until the next quarter sessions.

3 APRIL

1867 At Abingdon county bench Peter Ashfield, a blacksmith from East Hanney, was charged with beating his wife. Elisa Ashfield, who had brought the complaint, refused to press charges. She told magistrates that on reflection her husband only beat her when she deserved it. Justices warned Peter Ashfield about his unmanly actions and Elisa about wasting the court's time.

4 APRIL

1867 James Herbert, a brickmaker from Clewer, was charged with unmercifully assaulting and beating James Cox, a Clewer constable. At the hearing the charge was brought by Clewer's Head Constable, John Ballard, who stated that Constable Cox's injuries were so serious that he was unable to attend. The hearing was set for 10 May and at that time Herbert received a term of six months' hard labour.

5 APRIL

1882 At Maidenhead Borough Court Jane Beckem was charged with stealing a lady's jacket from a pawnbroker of that town. Shamal (the pawnbroker) stated that the prisoner came into his shop and asked to see some of the more expensive items that he kept in a safe at the back of his premises. On his return he saw the prisoner leaving his shop with a bulge under her

6 APRIL

Louisa Parsons, a young serving maid, lived at Mapledurham. She died in 1854 after attending a party at nearby Playhatch. Was she poisoned by a jealous friend? (*Author's Collection*)

blouse. It was some time later he noticed that a lady's jacket worth 30s was missing. He immediately sent his boy to Maidenhead police station. Constable Smith determined the prisoner's identity from Shamal's description. On knocking at the prisoner's door he was greeted by Beckem, dressed in the stolen jacket but with the braiding removed and the buttons altered. The magistrates found there was a case to be answered; the prisoner was remanded to the petty sessions, where at a later date Jane Beckem received three months' imprisonment.

7 APRIL **1866** At Newbury Borough Court a woman named Andrews, wife of Jason Andrews, landlord of the Steamer Inn, Cheap Street, was summoned for assault by Elizabeth Gingell. Sporting two black eyes, Gingell claimed that the affray was over rent. Andrews said that 'Squinting Lizzie' (Gingell) had consumed four quarts of strong ale for her breakfast and refused to pay for them. Both ladies were bound over to keep the peace.

8 APRIL **1163** De Montfort Island at Caversham was the scene of a 'trial by combat'. Before a massive crowd Robert De Montfort accused Henry De Essex of cowardice, both Knights of the Realm. It was common knowledge, before the English judicial system was established, that might was right. If, for instance, a man accused another of some misdeed, battle commenced. If the accused lost he was guilty, if he prevailed then he was innocent – a simple logic really.

The trouble began in 1157 when Henry II's army was pitched against the Welsh warrior prince, Owain Gwynedd. During the campaign, an elaborate and unsuccessful plan, initiated by the king himself, was put into action. The king, De Essex and De Montfort fled to Chester.

However, it was a full six years before De Montfort accused Essex of cowardice. Could it have been because King Henry had just appointed Essex as Constable of England, a position De Montfort had thought would be his? The battle lasted several hours with blood from many wounds spurting through the chain-mail of both combatants. Finally Essex collapsed to the ground and De Montfort leaned on his sword, totally spent, but aware he had proved his point.

King Henry had given permission for the loser, whomsoever it might be, but surely fatally wounded, to be interred in Reading Abbey. A litter was hastily constructed and the body borne across the river to the abbey gate. There Abbot Roger solemnly prepared the body for absolution, when, incredibly, a flicker of life was noticed under the bloodied sheet. Essex was alive. Nursed back to health over several months, Essex then joined the Benedictine Order at Reading. The fate of De Montfort is unknown.

9 APRIL **1942** At Reading Police Court in September, Maurice Victor Hogburn of Plough Lane, Wokingham, was accused of bigamy, having married Ellen Storey on 9 March while his wife Florence Hogburn was still alive. Florence Hogburn said that in 1935 she had gone down to Porlock for her health, taking their son with her. After staying six months she moved in with her parents at Caversham. She admitted that she had not seen her husband in nine years. Ellen Storey stated that she came from Worksop. In 1942 Hogburn came to lodge with her parents. He told her he was single and they became engaged; they married at Ilford on 9 April 1942. In October he told her he was already married. After much discussion they decided that Hogburn should go to the police and admit bigamy. The case was sent to the assizes where Hogburn received a three-month prison sentence.

1852 On this day Isaac Lee entered Bedlam (St Mary of Bethlehem) Asylum for the second and final time. Lee, who was retired from a small but profitable business, had suffered mental problems for some time. They seemed to stem from the death of his wife. The two had been inseparable, and her sudden death had been a heartfelt shock. After showing a strange and sometimes violent nature Isaac ended up in Bedlam.

In the 1850s it was possible for an inmate to be released from Bedlam if he could find responsible people to look after him. This being the case, Lee wrote to his sister and brother-in-law, Eliza and James Cannon of Boyne Hill, Maidenhead, requesting that he be permitted to lodge there. Knowing that Lee was tolerably affluent and after a reasonable rent had been agreed, Isaac soon became part of the Cannon household.

One day in late March 1852, four-year-old Lizzie Cannon was frolicking on the floor of her grandfather's house. Isaac Lee was watching her antics with fascination. Suddenly a piglet entered the room looking for scraps of food. For some unknown reason this simple action sent Isaac Lee into an uncontrollable blind fury. Seizing a nearby billhook Lee smashed it down on the piglet's head time and time again. Frightened by the piglet's screams and the vast quantities of blood, tiny Lizzie made for the door, but Lee barred her way. Shouting with anger he dealt with Lizzie in the same way as the piglet. After less than half a minute, the poor child lay bludgeoned to death. Constable Simon Frewin described at the Coroner's Court how he had been called to the horrific scene. He also stated that Lee was in a frenzy and that he needed the help of three stout neighbours to handcuff him. Lee was charged with murder at Reading but was found unfit to plead because of insanity. Isaac Lee spent the rest of his days in Bedlam.

1881 In the evening Mrs Reville, wife of Mr Reville, butcher of Slough, was found dead in her chair. She had died of horrifying wounds to her head and neck. The weapon, a meat cleaver, lay nearby, with a note saying: 'You won't sell me no more rotten meat.' It was signed by Mr Collins of Colnbrook. Superintendent Dunham went to question Collins, knowing it was very unlikely that the man was guilty. Collins, who admitted being a customer of the Reville's, was a highly respectable gentleman with a watertight alibi.

It did not take Dunham long to find a far more likely candidate for the murder. Alfred Paine, one of Reville's apprentices, had experienced a war of attrition with Mrs Reville who quite correctly suspected him of stealing and selling meat. Paine, the 16-year-old son of a local businessman, had worked

Hogarth's interpretation of Bedlam, from his series of satirical etchings the 'Rake's Progress'. Isaac Lee was incarcerated before and after the Boyne Hill tragedy of 1852.

late that night and had been witnessed leaving the premises at 8.50 p.m., the suspected time of the murder. Superintendent Dunham had his man 'banged to rights': not only did Paine have a motive there were also four reliable witnesses who saw him leaving the scene of the crime. The witnesses also described Paine as being in a highly agitated state. Added to this Dunham had found a handwriting expert who was prepared to swear that Paine had written the note himself. Better still, the half page it was written on was proven to have come from a notebook found on Paine's person.

'Why then?' asked the police. 'Why then?' asked Mr Reville. 'Why then?' asked the population of Slough. 'Why was it?' asked the local papers, 'that when Alfred Paine stood trial at Aylesbury, he was found not guilty?' Never had a verdict so contradicted the obvious. Never had a verdict flouted such a magnitude of evidence. It was obvious a murderer had walked free: could no one explain? In 1883 there was only one sentence possible for a convicted murderer and that was death. Age was not taken into account and there was no appeal system. Within a day or two of sentencing the perpetrator would mount the scaffold as sure as night followed day. Did the jury look at this poor guilt-ridden quivering boy and make a decision, however unpopular and illogical, to save his life? Who knows.

12 APRIL

1916 Maidenhead police officers raided 2 Norfolk Park Cottages and arrested George Thorpe, an Army deserter from the 9th King's Own Yorkshire Regiment, who should have been back in France on 8 March. Thorpe was handed over to the military authorities. Also arrested and charged with harbouring a deserter was Charles Carter, the owner of the property. Although Thorpe had a 'comfy little nest' in his attic, Carter stated in court that he had no idea he was there until he came across him lying in bed one morning (laughter in court). 'Come now Mr Carter,' stated the prosecuting solicitor. 'Are you telling the court that Thorpe lived in your house for over a month without you being aware of the fact?' 'I am a little hard of hearing,' stated the elderly Carter, 'and I seldom go upstairs.' Charles Carter went nowhere for some time. He received six months' hard labour.

1431 This is reputed to be the day that the free traders of Abingdon attacked the town's abbey. The abbey was resented by tradespeople because of the control it had and the taxes it extorted from them. This was the second rebellion, the first having been in 1327. A weaver named William Mandeville led this attack; it failed and he was executed.

13 APRIL

1748 John Williams, alias Thomas Watkins, was sentenced to death at Abingdon for highway robbery on Maidenhead Thicket. Unfortunately there is no information regarding when or even whether the sentence was carried out.

14 APRIL

1912 The sinking of the *Titanic*. Out of the 2,224 souls on board only 707 were saved. Among many Berkshire people that perished were Mrs Carter, niece to the Hughes brothers (the Revd John Hughes, vicar of Longcot, and his brother Thomas, author of *Tom Brown's Schooldays*), and her husband the Revd Carter.

15 APRIL

Many local personalities were among those who perished in the *Titanic* disaster in 1912. (*Illustrated London News*)

1938 On this day one of the last sightings of Herne the Hunter was recorded. Herne was reputed to be a hunter in Windsor Forest, and a favourite of Richard I, but owing to 'an accident' (reputedly a trap set by other jealous foresters) he lost both his sense of smell and hearing. Losing all favour he then lived the life of a recluse, dwelling in a mighty oak. He starved himself to death, and thereafter his ghost took revenge on the neighbours. Wearing antlers on his head, riding a fire-breathing mare and followed by a pack of hellhounds, Herne's spirit was regularly witnessed. This is one account of the Herne the Hunter stories, but there are many variations. Another is used in Shakespeare's *Merry Wives of Windsor*.

16 APRIL

1872 This was the day that Dr W.C. Minor was admitted to Broadmoor Asylum and became patient number 742 (see 17 February).

17 APRIL

1943 News was reported of a shooting in the bar of the New Inn in High Street, Bracknell. Emile le Corre (aged twenty-three) and Eugene Laot (aged twenty-one), both Free French soldiers, were involved in a heated argument that later turned into a brawl. At the request of the landlady, a Canadian serviceman ejected the pair, but trouble continued outside. Customers

18 APRIL

returning to the bar heard two shots ring out. On inspection they found Eugene Laot lying in the gutter with a bullet in his groin; of le Corre there was no sign. Le Corre was later apprehended and remanded to Kingston Assizes charged with grievous bodily harm.

19 APRIL **1930** Ascot's phantom policeman made another appearance. At his regular venue, a tight bend on the Virginia Water Road, a terrified motorist reported driving through a man with a tall hat and high collared tunic. As was his habit he turned, showing the frightened motorist his grossly deformed face.

20 APRIL **1838** On this day railway workers employed by Brunel's company rioted after a meeting at the Bull at Sonning. Two men were later sent to prison. Constable Charles Flower and a local blacksmith were commended for quelling the riot. The constable stated that it was no easy matter. He and the blacksmith had broken four staves in restoring order.

21 APRIL **1802** The *Windsor Gazette* expounded an upon 'extraordinary phenomenon'. At a Mapledurham farm a ewe belonging to Mr Pearman had given birth to a two-headed lamb. The extraordinary creature was placed under the protection of university scientist Richard Hill where it was kept in the highest state of preservation.

22 APRIL **1937** This was the day that Milo Brinn took over the Who'd A Tho't It, Nine Mile Ride, Saint Sebastian's, near Wokingham. The brewers were experiencing an outbreak of violence at the pub, so Milo Brinn, the retired strongman, was approached. Through the 1880s and '90s Brinn took his strongman act all over the world. Professor Attilla, the famous circus owner, saw Milo performing at the London Hippodrome and followed him to Paris's Folies Bergères. There the great showman signed up Milo and the partnership was successful for a decade. Attilla tried to persuade Milo to go to the United States with him in 1900 to start a strongman school, but Brinn was then in his early forties and decided to remain in England. He went on to set up an acrobatic group with his wife and children. Milo Brinn retired from the stage in 1937 at the age of seventy-three.

Milo Brinn, the strongman, took over the The Who'd A Tho't It, Nine Mile Ride, near Wokingham, in 1937. *(Maidenhead Adversiser)*

23 APRIL **1786** On this day Reading workmen dug up a box containing a severed hand. The member had been embalmed and was in good condition. It was presented to Reading Museum, but was later bought by a local philanthropist and donated to the Roman Catholic Church. The hand was thought to be that of St James who was executed in AD 44.

The Bull at Sonning, venue for a meeting of disgruntled railway workers on 20 April 1838. (*Brenda Allaway*)

1852 This was the day of the great Harwell fire. Nine farms, twenty-three cottages, hay, straw, livestock and farm produce were destroyed. George Murrell (aged seventeen) was seized on suspicion. He later confessed, but was known in the village to be of unsound mind. Murrell stated that another boy had given him a match and told him what to do. Residents of Harwell were later berated by the authorities for stealing each other's beds.

24 APRIL

1901 Ethel Mary Hardwick, wife of a Broadmoor Asylum attendant, who was also a reservist serving in South Africa, was charged at Wokingham Court with threatening to commit suicide. Dr Bradford of Easthampstead Institution (workhouse) where Hardwick and her three children were lodged, stated that Hardwick received both a Broadmoor and a War Office payment that amounted to £7 a month; there was definitely no reason to feel depressed. The prisoner was let off with a warning.

25 APRIL

1929 At 8.15 a.m. on this Saturday in April Alex Kirby, a milkman, knocked at the door of the Goldup's bungalow at Heywoods Park near Maidenhead. There was no reply, which slightly surprised Kirby as he knew the Goldups to be early risers. At 1.30 p.m. Kirby called again, his commission requiring prompt payment. He returned at 3.30 and finally at 6.30. On this last occasion, suspecting foul play, Kirby looked through the bedroom window. There appeared to be blood everywhere. Kirby fled to White Waltham police station returning with PC Frank Fraser. On forcing entry the officer found two bodies on a newly made blood-stained bed. The female had substantial head wounds and her throat had been cut; she was clearly dead. The male, although having sustained a deeply gashed throat, was still making deep moaning noises.

26 APRIL

At Oxford Assizes (Reading was too busy) on 7 June 1929 Percy Goldup was charged with the murder of his wife Jessie Goldup. The prisoner was a broken man and spent most of the trial in tears. After hearing a number of witnesses, all of whom referred to Goldup's mental instability, Mr Justice

Shearman stopped the trial and ordered the jury to bring in a verdict of guilty but insane. Percy Goldup spent the rest of his life in Broadmoor.

27 APRIL **1805** On this day in a court at Newbury John Hall was sentenced to seven years' transportation for stealing a rake and hoe; John Jiles three months' imprisonment for breaking a window; Ann Watts a week's hard labour for stealing two old horseshoes; Laura Cordray of Wokingham was sentenced to seven years' transportation for stealing two dresses; Thomas Jordan was gaoled for six months for indecent assault and the attempted rape of Elizabeth Wells. A hoe and rake were obviously valued to a far greater degree than Elizabeth Wells's chastity.

28 APRIL **1903** A divorce suit was granted to Robert Hardwick, a Broadmoor attendant and reservist. On his return from South Africa, Hardwick discovered his house repossessed, his three children in Easthampstead Institution and his wife in bed with a man from Reading named Deakin. Ethel Hardwick (see the 25th) had also acquired a six-week-old child during Robert's absence.

29 APRIL **1922** On this day Thomas Henry Allaway was reputedly arrested near a Reading bookmakers. Allaway, a chauffeur from Bournemouth, was wanted for the murder of Irene Wilkins on 21 December 1921. Miss Wilkins had advertised for a job in the *Morning Post*. The same day she received a reply telling her to catch a train down to Bournemouth where she would be met by car. The following day her body was found dumped in a field on the edge of the town. Tyre tracks suggested the car was one belonging to a local businessman and driven by his chauffeur, Thomas Allaway. Two other telegrams were also found luring Irene Wilkins to Bournemouth; each had similar spelling mistakes. What police needed was an example of Allaway's handwriting. This they received in an unusual way when he attempted to pass a cheque on which he had forged his employer's signature. Allaway attempted a getaway; he vanished from Bournemouth but was detained at Reading. Found guilty by a jury and then finally admitting his guilt, 36-year-old Allaway took the drop at Winchester on 19 August 1922.

30 APRIL **1786** On this day Mr Broom of Kennington awoke his wife Jane abruptly, bound and gagged her and transported her to Littlemore in Berkshire. There he sold her for 5*s* to a man named Pantin, who led her away with a halter around her neck. Pantin later gave away his possession to a woodman at Bagley Woods.

Broad Street, Reading, in 1922. Here Bournemouth chauffeur Thomas Allaway was arrested. He was later charged with the murder of Irene Wilkins. *(Berkshire County Library)*

MAY

The haunting figure of Henry Pounds Watts disappeared when
his son's cross was re-erected. Alan Watts died in May 1879.
(Brenda Allaway)

1 MAY **1770** On this May Day in St Nicholas, Hurst, a local lass named Molly Tape hanged herself. Molly fell in love with Dick Darvill, a local farmer who played the field. Molly was known to be a little on the promiscuous side herself, but when she met Dick it was love at first sight. Dick was to be the total and exclusive target of her affection. Darvill, however, found it hard to curb his philandering. Molly found out she had competition and in a fit of pique hanged herself from a beech tree in what came to be known locally as Tape Lane.

For some unknown reason Molly's scantily clad ghost has regularly been witnessed near the village pond. One reported sighting was in Easter 1971. Molly's spectre, apparently dressed in a pair of briefs, caused sufficient interest for the local media to become involved. This in turn led to a succession of jokers in blonde wigs and sporting briefs running around Hurst pond in the moonlight. Finally a priest was called to conduct an exorcism; the jokers turned their talents elsewhere and poor Molly was laid to rest.

2 MAY **1911** The best way to relate what happened at a Wokingham forge on this day is to summarise the words of Charles White at Reading Assizes on 6 June. George Barker was in the dock indicted for feloniously killing his brother

Molly Tape's ghost appeared at Hurst pond. The attractive village girl remained true to her intended, Dick Darvill, but he regularly strayed, which drove her to commit suicide in 1770. *(Brenda Allaway)*

Henry. White stated that he was the only full-time employee at the Barkers' forge in Station Road, Wokingham. There were also two part-time employees but neither was present on that fatal May day. Charles White stated that the three of them were working good humouredly that day. At 11 a.m., as usual, George Barker went next door to the Hope and Anchor and returned with some beer. While they were taking refreshment a discussion arose during which George mildly berated Henry for letting a customer he didn't trust have further credit. The row became heated and George made for the door in an attempt to call upon the customer and demand money. Henry was intent on stopping him; he was a great believer in customer relations. Henry barred the way, George grabbed him and the pair rolled together in the forge yard.

The small entrance to the Barkers' forge, where Henry Barker died in 1911 after a row with his brother, George. Joseph Capon, landlord of the Hope and Anchor pub next door, gave evidence. *(Brenda Allaway)*

Ann Barker, mother of the two combatants, came into the yard a few minutes later. Henry lay on his back complaining about a terrible pain in his leg and shaking uncontrollably. Dr Bokenham was called and he in turn alerted PC Burke. Henry was rushed to the Royal Berkshire Hospital but died during the journey. In court Dr Bokenham stated that Henry had suffered a broken leg and delirium tremens that together had brought on a heart attack. At this point the judge called the lawyers to his bench. After this consultation he announced to the jury that there was no case to answer.

1835 A Berkshire paper reported the terrifying experiences of two brothers at Woolhampton. William and Charles Hazell of Midgham were travelling in their gig near Woolhampton when they were assailed by four men. Despite courageous endeavours by Charles and his whip, all resistance ceased when one of the villains placed a pistol at his brother's head. The brothers were secured and a sum of £14 or £15 was stolen. A reward of £10 was offered for the rogue's apprehension.

3 MAY

1867 Several Newbury landlords who had been keeping rather flexible hours spent this day in court. William Kimber of The Jolly Millers was accused of keeping his beerhouse open between 3 and 5 p.m. on Good Friday. A constable had looked in and seen four people drinking. He had then proceeded

4 MAY

The Narrow Boat (once the White House), where landlord Alfred Billing was fined £1 for serving drinks after time in 1867. (*Brenda Allaway*)

to the White House where he witnessed six people drinking with the landlord, Alfred Billing. Kimber was fined 10s plus 10s costs; Billing was fined £1 plus 10s costs.

5 MAY **1857** Mary Smith (aged twenty-four) made three attempts to pass a counterfeit coin at Maidenhead. Apprehended by Constable Sexton, Smith was remanded to Reading County Court where she received six months' imprisonment.

6 MAY **1857** Henry Payne was committed for trial at the next Reading sessions. Payne was 'taken' by Edward Conroy Esq that morning, charged with stealing a smock frock coat which belonged to Mr Peart of Barkham. Taken to Reading by the Barkham constable, Payne fled from the gates of the gaol.

7 MAY **1943** This day brought the news that a missing Reading schoolgirl had been found. The thirteen-year-old had been missing from her home for three days. Her description had been circulated and also that of her clothing, in particular a green coat. WPC Brunch noticed a girl dressed in green and fitting the description on Westminster Bridge Road. On inquiry the young lady seemed in no pains to deny her identity.

8 MAY **1850** At Reading county court, Jeremy Parker and John Walker (tramps) were charged with having 18lb of lead in their possession. Each was sentenced to twenty-one days' hard labour. Joshua Wicks was charged with damage to a street light and given fourteen days' hard labour. On the same day James Coxhead, described as a noisy hawker and desperate character, was accused of assaulting Anne Parsons, a cripple, in Silver Street, Reading. The assault took place at a fair booth where both parties had barrows.

Anne Parsons and other witnesses stated that Coxhead had used foul language and pushed over her barrow. The case was proven and Coxhead was fined 10s or seven days in Bridewell.

1759 This is reputed to be the day that Hannah Snell married at Newbury. Keeping her gender secret Hannah had served as a dragoon in the Army and also in the Navy. There are several rhymes about her. Hannah died in 1792 at Chelsea Hospital. She spent her declining years there and is buried in the gardens. **9 MAY**

1879 Esther Chamberlain, who had escaped from Reading gaol on 2 May, was recaptured. Her cell in E wing had been found empty; she had slipped the bolt in the cell and disappeared over the wall with no keys or outside help. On 10 May a constable recognised the prisoner at Goring-on-Thames and effected an arrest. **10 MAY**

1857 On this day in Reading, George Higgs, an apprentice at Williams's ironmongers, charged Josephus Collis, a freeman working at the same establishment, with assault. Higgs had informed Williams, so the story goes, that Collis was doing his own work in Williams's time. After being severely berated by the owner, Collis followed Higgs to the Shoulder of Mutton at **11 MAY**

James Coxhead, a desperate character, assaulted crippled Anne Parsons at her market stall in Silver Street, Reading, in 1850. *(Berkshire County Library)*

The Shoulder of Mutton, Dunsden, where Josephus Collis 'severely pulled and twisted' George Higgs's nose in 1857. (*Brenda Allaway*)

Dunsden. There, after a slight altercation, Collis severely pulled and twisted the apprentice's nose. The defendant was fined 1*s* with 9*d* costs.

12 MAY **1879** On a back road between Marlborough and Hungerford there is a very steep incline. A local newspaper notified the public of a horrendous accident. It stated that as a carter's three-horse team was descending with the owner and his boy at the head (the correct position), the horses suddenly took flight, throwing the carter and lad, fourteen-year-old Alan Watts, to the ground. Unfortunately the wagon, which was loaded with coal, ran over young Alan's body. There was no hope for him: with every rib and many other bones shattered he died two hours later. Local people of Mildenhall and Axford paid to have a small cross erected at the place of Alan Watts's accident. Over the years it became covered with brambles and other foliage. When the council cleared the site, the cross and other debris were tossed to the top of the small valley.

In 1956 a family driving along the route on a misty evening saw a silent and subdued figure standing in the road. He wore a long coat and a bowler hat and was clean-shaven. There being no way round him, the driver and passengers got out of the car. As they did so the tall figure turned and vanished. Although shaken the party resumed their journey. The story was treated with much scepticism until several older villagers remembered Henry Pounds Watts, father of Alan. Watts had lived in the village for many years until his death in 1907. Henry was unique in appearance, very tall and gaunt and sporting no facial hair, which was unheard of in those days. Local papers recounted this sighting and what had happened to the memorial, whereupon the cross was found and re-erected. Finally, father and son lay at rest.

13 MAY

1881 This is supposedly the date on which an unnamed young serving girl disappeared near Lambourn Place, Lambourn. The house was the home of the last of the Hippisley clan. Henry Hippisley was not a popular man; although he was feared for his ruthless power, the villagers had occasionally found the courage to oppose him. Once Hippisley had removed timber fan-vaulting from the local church to help in the construction of the new Lambourn Place. Nothing was done to stop him and the villagers were left seething at the insult. On a second occasion Henry was prosecuted for defrauding the local almshouse; an inadequate fine followed.

Personifying as he did the all-powerful landowner, Hippisley also decided that any local maiden was a perk of the job and many ashamed maids were known to have suffered a deflowering at his hands. One disappeared after working at the house. It was suggested by the villagers that Henry had killed her in a fit of temper when she would not countenance his demands. Although hundreds of acres of Lambourn Woods were searched no body was found. No body; no murder; no charge. If there was a secret, Henry Hippisley took it to the grave with him in 1890.

14 MAY

1856 On this day John Blackwell, late of the Berkshire Militia, returned from Corfu. Blackwell came to stay with his grandfather, William Blackwell, at Rose Street in Wokingham. There he supplemented his income by doing odd jobs and gardening.

It was known that John Blackwell had witnessed some horrific sights in his military service, and it was thought that the tranquillity of the rural town would suit him fine. His work was not arduous, his home life calming and he made a friend of Thomas Rance, a neighbour who took him fishing. Nothing untoward happened until 11 June 1856 when John Blackwell was enjoying tea with his grandfather and some elderly neighbours. Suddenly he jumped up, screaming, 'I must die, I am going to die'. Blackwell was led to his room and Dr Norris was called. The doctor supplied limited medication that seemed to calm the patient. On Tuesday 12 June Blackwell's condition had deteriorated badly, his abuse far more vehement. On Wednesday William Blackwell had hidden all the knives and suggested that his elderly female lodger remained in her room. Later in the afternoon Mr Beechy, a medical specialist, stated that if John did not improve by the morning he would commit him to Littlemore.

Wokingham police arresting a suspect. The man on the right is thought to be PC Porter, one of the officers responsible for arresting the 'Wokingham Messiah' in 1856. *(Berkshire County Library)*

Morning did not come for poor Thomas Rance who had been looking after John Blackwell. The crazed young man's demented mind had convinced him that he was the Messiah and Rance was the Devil. Words to this effect were screamed by the nightshirt-clad Blackwell as he dashed from Rose Street to the town hall, eluding policemen and the residents.

At 3 a.m. on 14 June Henry Paty was sitting in his parlour in Rose Street, after the general chaos and hullabaloo had woken him. There was a tap on his back window and he cautiously admitted John Blackwell. Blackwell was weeping as he inquired about the condition of his friend Thomas Rance. On being informed that Tommy was dead Blackwell, full of contrition, permitted Paty to deliver him into the arms of PC Porter. On 11 July 1856 John Blackwell was charged at Reading with the murder of Thomas Rance. It was decided that Blackwell was insane and therefore incapable of pleading. He was sent to Littlemore by the Secretary of State.

15 MAY   **1939** George Henry Willis was charged at Reading with the horrendous murder of Frederick Paul, an 85-year-old self-employed gardener who sold his meagre produce on Windsor Bridge. Paul's body was discovered in a small pool behind his one-roomed shanty in Winkfield. The body was half-submerged with only the head and shoulders discernible. The skull and part of the neck had been blasted away leaving vast gaps in his face. Paul's pockets had been cut and the motive was thought to be robbery. After the accumulation of much circumstantial evidence George Willis was arrested at his home in Ascot. At Reading Assizes witnesses placed him near the scene of the crime. There was also much controversial evidence about whether or not the shot was of a sort used by Willis. However, the whole case seemed to rest on a pair of scissors with flattened ends. They were sworn to belong to Paul but were found on Willis's person. Willis stated they had been his for years

The Tally Ho at Winkfield, where shots were heard on the night Frederick Paul was murdered. It is now a private house. (*Brenda Allaway*)

and that he used them to mend watches. Surrounded by a full court, with the shadow of the gallows hanging over him, Willis asked counsel for his watch. He then proceeded to remove three tiny screws. George Willis walked free.

1936 On this day a humble farmer was due to take the drop at Birmingham. The farmer, 68-year-old Thomas Townsend, lived with his wife Elizabeth, his daughter Mary (aged seventeen) and Elizabeth's son from a previous marriage, Godfrey Parker (aged twenty), in a small cottage at Lambourn. Thomas, 5ft 4in tall and of slight build, was not an ambitious man; a simple life and a few bob for beer was all he craved. Not so his wife Lizzie, twenty years his junior; she was a workaholic with plans. Lizzie was virtually keeping the family while Thomas, who was retired, spent most of his time in the pub. After a Saturday afternoon with her daughter in Newbury Lizzie returned home. Much later Thomas returned from the George, where he found his wife and Godfrey in muted conversation. On Thomas's arrival the pair went upstairs to continue their whispering. Thomas waited angrily. When his wife came back down there was an angry scene that culminated in Lizzie hammering on the door of a close neighbour, Miss Cartwright. Miss Cartwright finally managed to open the door and admit Lizzie Townsend but was too late to prevent the entrance of her demented husband. There was a flash and a bang and Lizzie collapsed in the doorway, her shoulder blasted away by shot. She died several hours later.

16 MAY

A preliminary hearing into the death of Frederick Paul was held at Windsor Guildhall, a most unsuitable and inconvenient place. (*Michael Stiles*)

LAMBOURN STABBING AFFRAY

JOCKEY CHARGED WITH UNLAWFUL WOUNDING

MAN TAKEN TO HOSPITAL WITH JACK-KNIFE IN THE NECK

STATED TO BE DANGEROUSLY ILL

On 16 May 1936 Thomas Townsend (aged sixty-eight) was due to hang for the murder of his wife Lizzie at their cottage in Lambourn. Coincidentally, there had been another slaying at the same cottage six years earlier when Frederick Giddings was stabbed by local jockey Derrick Cheshire. *(Newbury Library)*

Thomas Townsend was found hiding under rags in a nearby barn. In March, at a Birmingham court, Townsend stood in the dock seeming not to understand what was going on. His barrister claimed that he had the mind of a young child. Townsend was found guilty and sentenced to death. There was an unsuccessful appeal heard by the Lord Chief Justice but finally, at the eleventh hour, Townsend was reprieved. He spent the rest of his life in Winston Green and Broadmoor.

Incidentally, lightning may not strike twice, but violent death certainly does. At the same house six years previously a violent confrontation had erupted between two sets of neighbours, the Cheshires and the Giddings. The affray ended when Derrick Cheshire, under attack by the Giddings brothers with stake posts, stabbed Fred Giddings. When the weapon was removed at Newbury Hospital Giddings was paralysed down one side. He died a week later of septic pneumonia. Derrick James Cheshire was committed to Birmingham Assizes for trial. At the end of the trial the jury took six minutes to decide that Cheshire had killed in self-defence; he walked free.

17 MAY **1852** An inquest was held at the Green Dragon, Maidenhead, on Richard Whittle (aged sixty-two), a stonemason from Preston. Whittle had become abusive in the bar on 10 May, kicking and biting and striking out at other customers. He offered to take one man, named Abercrombie, outside. The man went reluctantly, others joined them and fighting broke out. Whittle eventually returned to the bar and then bedded down in the stable. In the morning he was dead. The Coroner's Court found the cause of death to be compression of the brain caused by a blow or fall, but as a result of what no one could tell.

18 MAY **1824** On this day a local paper blandly stated that William Charles was hanged at Reading for offering a £5 note. There is no other information on the case.

19 MAY **1892** This was the day that the Revd Robert J.K. Bell was accused of indecent assault on two young ladies while travelling by rail between Kintbury and Bedwin. Fanny Claire Abery (aged sixteen) later stated that she and her friend had been touched by Bell in delicate places. At the quarter sessions Fanny's friend did not wish to press charges, but Fanny did. There was insufficient evidence and Bell was found not guilty. The newspapers from that time strongly implied that Fanny had a crush on the attractive young Revd Bell.

1833 A pork butcher of Thames Street, Windsor, was fined for emptying pails of filth from his 'blood hole' into the street. The butcher's name was Hywill Swill.

1836 Four new constables were sworn in at Maidenhead in order to deal with the abundance of beggars. The main task of this burly team was to apprehend tramps and beggars and bring them in. It is not specified whether they were to be dead or alive.

1937 Strange witchcraft signs were found in the village of Whistley Green, near Hurst. Trees and walls had been daubed with symbols and chanting was heard in the early evening. The villagers' association with witchcraft persisted over the decades. In May 1960 a deserted cottage held the remains of some ritualistic mass. Figures with stag horns and bull horns were painted on the ceiling along with any amount of disquieting and deformed figures. The perpetrators were never discovered.

In 1960 a derelict cottage in Whistley Green was found to contain many paintings and articles associated with the practice of witchcraft. (*Brenda Allaway*)

1439 In this year it was announced that the recent Black Death had depopulated the town of Wallingford to such an extent that only forty-four households were left. New roads were being constructed to bypass the town. Travellers avoided it like the plague!

1624 Eighteen press-ganged prisoners held at Compton Prison, Reading, revolted on this date. The conditions in the old gaol opposite St Lawrence's Church were appalling. At this time Greyfriars Church was also used as a House of Correction for the old, orphans, the poor and petty criminals. From both places prisoners were led away to be punished in the Market Place, where a whipping post, stocks and a pillory stood. All were used on a regular basis.

1907 A gentleman named Haley was charged with being drunk and incapable at Little Sandhurst. PC Dobson stated that he had actually seen the prisoner fall from his bike into a ditch. Haley, however, was adamant that he was sober and had been knocked off his bike by a car. PC Dobson then found witnesses to state that only two cars had been seen in Little Sandhurst that day and neither of them near the scene of the incident. The case was proven and Haley was fined 12*s* 6*d*.

1937 Inmates were still dying regularly in Broadmoor Asylum. On 26 May an inquest was held on Alice Ada Money (aged seventy-four). Alice had been admitted in 1903 when, while employed as a governess, she had grievously wounded one of her charges. The inquest found that Alice had died of pneumonia. A second inquest followed shortly after concerning the death of Charles Trout. Trout a farm labourer, had been convicted in 1903 for the attempted murder of a farmer at Exeter. The inquest found that the death was due to myocardial degeneration.

27 MAY **1863** Dr John Meyer began his term as the first Physician Superintendent of Broadmoor Asylum. His deputy was Dr W. Orange and the chaplain was the Revd J.T. Burt.

28 MAY **1863** This day brought an influx of patients to Broadmoor Asylum. The first to arrive were ninety-five women from Bethlem and Fisherton House.

29 MAY **1976** On this day the local newspapers reported on Maidenhead's 'Battle of the Boyne'. Mabel Withers of 18 Boyne Hill charged neighbour Margaret Crighton with assault. Withers stated that she was taking the clothes off the line for her neighbour, Mrs Ceres, at no. 20. It was raining and she was doing her friend a good turn. Crighton came out into her garden and started shouting abuse, accusing her of being mad and doing away with her children. To further aggravate matters Crighton threw some newly dug muddy earth at her. Withers retaliated with a bucket of dirty water. Hair pulling followed. The mayor, summing up, found both parties at fault. Both ladies were bound over and had to share the £5 costs.

Chain Street in Reading where Jane Cox had a room in 1896; did she murder her baby here? (Brenda Allaway)

30 MAY **1896** On this night at 11.30 p.m. an extremely pregnant shop assistant went to bed in her small room in Chain Street, Reading. Jane Cox was twenty-one

and lived above her workplace; below lived the owners of the shop, John and Susan Drake. Mrs Drake was downstairs darning and awaiting her husband's return. On hearing a moaning and groaning upstairs Susan rushed to see if she could be of assistance. The sight that met the young wife's eyes was appalling. There was blood everywhere – the floor, the bedclothes and all over the transfixed Jane Cox. Susan Drake shouted to her returning husband to get medical assistance. This he did, fetching a local surgeon Mr Key. The surgeon soon ascertained that the child had been born complete and had been severely mutilated afterwards. Jane Cox was arrested, but in June she was found not guilty of infanticide. It was obvious that some sort of deal had been brokered in which Jane agreed to get psychiatric help. She spent the remainder of her days in Broadmoor.

31 MAY **1624** This is reputed to be the day that two ale tasters, employed by Reading Corporation to check for watered beer, were sacked for favouritism.

JUNE

Protesting suffragettes were a constant thorn in the side for Berkshire police between 1910 and 1914.
(Illustrated London News)

In 1914 Wargrave church was the victim of arson, believed, though never proved, to have been the work of suffragettes. *(Brenda Allaway)*

1 JUNE **1914** At 2.30 a.m. a massive blaze could be seen in the sky above Wargrave. There had been an arson attack on St Mary's Church. Wargrave engine and pump were first to arrive at 3.20 a.m. and the Henley pump soon afterwards. Although heroic attempts were made, only the Norman tower remained standing. Many irreplaceable artefacts had also been destroyed. The police questioned members of the public and focused their attentions on a local suffragette group. The officers had no doubt whatsoever that the fire had been started deliberately.

2 JUNE **1922** Jack Hewitt, a fifteen-year-old lad, was arraigned at Oxford Assizes. He was charged with the horrific murder of Sarah Blake, the landlady of the Crown and Anchor pub at Gallows Tree Common, near Reading. Sarah Blake had been found by her charlady at 8.30 a.m. on 4 March. Her injuries were horrendous; blood was splattered on doors, cupboards and even the ceiling. The landlady had been beaten and stabbed with the ferocity of a lunatic before having her throat cut.

This knife, used by Jack Hewitt to murder Sarah Blake in 1922, was found in a hedge near the Crown and Anchor. (Both sides of the kife are shown.) *(Henley Library)*

Jack Hewitt had been sent to the inn to fetch beer for his father early the previous evening. He was gone some time and on returning stated that the inn was closed and that he had had to go to the Reformation a short distance on. Several of Mrs Blake's potential customers that evening confirmed that the inn had been shut. Hewitt was in the frame from very early on, but several men were brought in for questioning. Progress was also impeded by a Reading man named Sheppard who falsely admitted to the crime.

A breakthrough came when the murder weapon was found in a nearby hedge by a local constable. Witnesses stated that the knife was Hewitt's and it was sent to the Home Office along with Hewitt's brown stained tunic, a doorknocker, blood-soaked paper and Sarah Blake's woollen shawl. Hewitt was arrested and admitted the crime at Caversham police station. He had gone to the pub earlier and had been given strawberry champagne and ginger beer by the kindly landlady. Then for reasons he could not explain, he had picked up a metal bar used for shifting barrels and struck her over the head. He followed this act with numerous stabbings before finally cutting his victim's throat. At Oxford it took the jury only half an hour to find Hewitt guilty. Mr Justice Shearman regretted that he could not give the death penalty to one so young. Jack Hewitt was to be detained at His

Jack Hewitt, who murdered Sarah Blake at Gallows Tree Common. *(Henley Library)*

Majesty's pleasure. When asked why he had committed this terrible crime Hewitt answered, 'Blame it on the pictures'. Was he the first to be affected by violence at the cinema?

1919 On this day Eton College announced that 1,157 Etonians had died in the First World War. In addition, 900 had been decorated, and 13 had received the Victoria Cross.

3 June

1757 On this date Wokingham was being plagued by a spate of burglaries. Samuel Walden, a shopkeeper at the town's Market Place, had had his premises burgled and many articles of various kinds stolen. On the same night Mrs Dean Burgess had found a hock of bacon missing from the town's laundry, Mrs Clempson of Denmark Street had lost a nightshirt from her spare bedroom, and a pail of milk had disappeared from a house in Rose Street.

4 June

1832 Henry Mullins, a well-known criminal, escaped from Reading gaol. Mullins hid in his cell while the other inmates went to chapel, escaping later down a builder's hole. He was never heard of again. Thomas Webb, who was the turnkey responsible for searching the cells, was charged with negligence of duty and was publicly reprimanded.

5 June **1791** A serving maid, who had been caught shoplifting in Newbury, was sentenced to be led around tied to a donkey cart and to be whipped in the town's main streets. Afterwards she was to spend three months in solitary confinement.

6 June **1882** Dr Orange, Physician Superintendent of Broadmoor Asylum, was attacked in his office. The patient, a 56-year-old clergyman, struck Dr Orange across the head as he worked at his desk. The weapon was found to be a rock wrapped in a handkerchief. Dr Orange was away from his duties for six weeks and the attack was partly responsible for his early retirement.

7 June **1916** At Reading Borough Court Ernest Kirkland, a fruiterer, was charged with being drunk in charge of a horse and cart. Two constables reported that on 2 June a young lady pulled up in a car. She stated that she had been greatly perturbed by a horse and cart that had pulled out of a side street. She had narrowly missed a collision and had then been the recipient of a long stream of foul language. At this moment Kirkland drove by and was identified by the lady. The constables blew their whistles but Kirkland seemed unwilling or unable to stop. After peddling after the accused for some distance the two constables finally managed to apprehend him and found that he was unable to stand. He was transferred to Reading police station where Dr Malochnochie diagnosed Kirkland as having acute alcohol poisoning. The mayor fined the accused £2 with 10s 6d costs.

8 June **1864** On this day Mary McBride claimed the distinction of being the first woman to escape from Broadmoor Asylum. She was recaptured in Reading the following day.

9 June **1912** An investigation was held at Newbury concerning some very old inhabitants who stated that within living memory three Berkshire witches had been buried alive. The incident had taken place at Cottington's Hill, a mile south of Kingsclere.

The elderly witnesses stated that the witches had been buried up to their necks and left to starve. One witch outlived her sisters because somebody had thrown her an apple, which she had managed to catch in her mouth. Why any credibility was given to such a story in the comparatively enlightened twentieth century is a mystery. There are, however, many such mysterious stories around the Newbury district. Probably the most famous tells of a witch who was captured and executed by Cromwell's soldiers in 1643. According to a pamphlet of the time the soldiers saw an old woman sailing down the River Kennett on a plank. The witch was seized and shot but she caught the bullets, put them in her mouth and chewed them. One of the soldiers, who was well up on such matters, knew that it was possible to kill the most troublesome of witches by slashing their foreheads. This he proceeded to do and just for good measure he let off a pistol beside her ear. It seems that the method was infallible because she sank at his feet and died (see p. 6).

(see p. 6).

1896 On this day Amelia Elizabeth Dyer, Reading's abhorred baby farmer, was hanged at Newgate. Billington, the famous hangman, had fixed her arms in such a way as to prevent her 16-stone frame pulling her head off. Mrs Dyer had been convicted at Reading on a charge of murdering tiny Edith Marmon, a child in her care. It was a test case, as Edith was one of two recognisable bodies, the other being a small boy named Simonds.

Edith Marmon was the illegitimate daughter of a pretty Cheltenham barmaid named Evalina Marmon. After reading a newspaper advertisement Evalina travelled to Reading in January 1896 to leave her daughter in the hands of 'Mrs Stanfield', a friendly and devout woman. The cost for boarding the child was £10.

Ever since the previous summer many horrifying discoveries had been made in the Thames at London. Over forty babies' bodies, in various stages of decomposition, had been found. None was stillborn; all had been strangled. Less than a month after 'Mrs Stanfield' had taken in Edith more gruesome discoveries were emerging at Reading. Six more small bodies had been found, three in the Thames, one in the Kennett and two at a place known as Clappers Pool. All had been strangled with red tape that was attached to a brick. The first body found in the Thames at Reading was pulled up accidentally by a bargee. He brought up his pole to find a parcel at the end with a baby's arm hanging out. On the sodden brown paper a name and address was still discernible: 'Mrs Dyer, Kensington Road, Reading'.

One of the vilest criminals of the Victorian age was Amelia Dyer. She was hanged at Newgate on 10 June 1896. Billington, the famous hangman, fixed her arms to stop her 16-stone body pulling her head off. (*Berkshire County Library*)

Detective Inspector Anderson, who was in charge of the case, rushed officers to the house. The bird had flown, but only across the river to Caversham where she was arrested. Anderson found so much evidence at each abode that he soon had a watertight case. Two children, who for some reason had been permitted to live, gave evidence, as did Dyer's daughter and son-in-law. There were also many other witnesses. Against such odds Amelia Elizabeth Dyer found it prudent to plead guilty but insane. The jury were having none of it. One of Victorian Britain's most offensive women was despatched at Newgate.

1932 On this day came a twist in the worldwide coverage of the Lindbergh kidnapping. On 1 March 1932 Colonel Charles Lindbergh, ace aviator and internationally known pilot, who five years before flew from New York to

LINDBERGH BABY FOUND DEAD NEAR HOME; MURDERED SOON AFTER THE KIDNAPPING 72 DAYS AGO AND LEFT LYING IN WOODS

POLICE INTENSIFY HUNT

Curtis, Norfolk Agent, and Condon, Who Paid Ransom, at Hopewell.

TO AID PROSECUTOR TODAY

Schwarzkopf Says Restraints Designed to Safeguard Baby Now Can Be Thrown Off.

A GROUP UNDER SUSPICION

Gov. Moore Pledges Relentless Hunt — Mulrooney Also Promises Full Aid.

WHERE KIDNAPPERS LEFT SLAIN BABY.

BODY MILE FROM HOPEWELL

Discovered by Chance Near Centre of Wide Search for Child.

HALF-COVERED BY LEAVES

Skull Fractures Caused Death —Body and Clothing Are Identified by Nurse.

MOTHER IS BRAVE AT NEWS

Neighbors Had Complained That Hunt in Vicinity Had Not Been Thorough.

Newbury's Violet Sharpe, the Lindbergh family's parlour-maid, committed suicide on 11 June 1934. She had been interrogated once and was about to be questioned again.

Paris in 33½ hours, came home to his mansion in Hopewell, New Jersey. Lindbergh arrived at 8:30 p.m. An hour and a half later at 10.01 p.m. nurse Gow found Charles Jnr missing from his cot and informed his mother, Anne Lindbergh. At 10.05 p.m. Lindbergh found a ransom note for $50,000. The crime was thought to have inside connections. On 4 March Lindbergh offered to deal with the kidnappers. On 5 March the ransom was raised to $70,000. On 8 March a mysterious Dr Condon offered to act as a go-between. On 12 May the body of the Lindbergh baby was found. (There has long been some doubt as to whether or not this was the actual body or a substitute.)

Local interest arises through Violet Sharpe, a highly strung 28-year-old Newbury girl, who worked as the Lindbergh's parlour-maid. At her first interview with the police she informed them she had been at the cinema that evening. Later Violet changed her story and stated she had been picked up by a man. On 21 May, nearly three months after the kidnapping, Miss Sharpe made further conflicting statements, and, after being told on 10 June that the police intended yet another interview, she committed suicide. Her body was found on 11 June.

On 19 September 1934 a German named Bruno Richard Hauptmann was arrested. Ransom money was found at his house. On 2 January 1935 Bruno Hauptmann was charged with murder at the County Court house at Flemington, New Jersey. A guilty verdict was reached on 13 February and on 3 April 1936 Hauptmann was executed at Trenton State Prison, New Jersey. There has always been serious doubt about his guilt.

12 June **1863** The local media informed its readers that Thomas Mullins, a brutal convict, had escaped from Broadmoor Asylum. Mullins had evaded a warder

and eluded a strict search for him. He was thirty-three, 5ft 5in tall and nearing the end of a four-year sentence. Mullins was arguably the first man to escape from Broadmoor. He came from a villainous family; his father, Thomas Mullins Snr, had been hanged five years previously for the murder of Miss Elmsley. The case became known nationally as the 'Stepney murder'.

1784 On this day it came to light that Mr Rose, a brewer, was killed in a duel with Dick England at Ascot races. Unfortunately little more is known of the affair – perhaps Mr England didn't care for Mr Rose's beer.

13 June

1910 Mr Hicks of Crowthorne Farm was prosecuted for letting a bull stray on to the highway. Mrs Rut stated that in mid-May she saw the bull blocking the road near the farm. It bellowed three times then came straight at her. She escaped injury by striking the beast on the head and then hiding behind a tree. Mr Hicks stated that the animal was a mere calf and only wanted to be friendly. He was fined *2s 6d*.

1781 At this time the good citizens of Reading were a little concerned about Dr Richard Valpy, the headmaster of Reading School. The town wondered if Valpy, 'a mighty flogger' nicknamed 'Dr Wackerbach', was taking discipline a little too far. Valpy had taken over Reading School when it was in an extremely depressed state. In 1790 he rebuilt it at his own expense. He wrote his own schoolbooks that were adopted by many schools, and his adaptation of Shakespeare's *King John* was performed at Covent Garden. Valpy's academic success at Reading School was legendary. 'So what if he was a bit of a martinet, it got results didn't it?' No more was said.

14 June

1867 On this day at Newbury petty sessions John Pocock was summoned for assaulting Edmund Scarrett at Curridge. Scarrett, landlord of the New Inn, said that he and some friends were having a drink on Whit Monday afternoon when he heard a quarrel break out in the bar parlour. On entering he found Pocock lashing out with his fists and using abusive language. Scarrett tried to remonstrate with Pocock but received a blow to the mouth, which sent him over the back of his settle. Complete uproar followed. When police officers arrived they found Pocock outside the inn, threatening a group of people with an iron stake post. Pocock was fined *6s* with *14s* costs.

15 June

1899 At Berkshire Assizes Joseph Slatter (aged forty-six) and Robert James (aged thirty-one) appeared on a manslaughter charge. The trouble all began at Eastertide, when the two men entered the Chequers in the village of Harwell. Isaac Day, the landlord, had already barred James whom he knew to be a thief and a man with a violent streak when inebriated.

16 June

Day watched the two getting steadily drunker and more abusive to his customers. Fearing worse to come, Day despatched his pot boy to PC Hewett, the village constable. As the boy arrived he found Hewett chin-wagging on his doorstep with John Charlton, a young constable from neighbouring East

Hendred. Back at the Chequers the situation was deteriorating fast. Abused customers were leaving and Isaac Day was confronting Slatter and James when both constables arrived. Their very presence seemed initially to calm things, but as they chatted to the landlord a violent quarrel erupted in the taproom. Hewett walked towards the taproom door after sending Charlton around to meet them at the outside door.

Hewett decided on swift action; he and the landlord grabbed a combatant each and ejected them into the village street. Abuse and threats followed the two men as they returned to the pub. It was at this precise moment that Charlton came around the corner of the inn. James ran and head-butted the young constable, driving him to the ground and cracking his skull on a kerbstone. James and Slatter then kicked him mercilessly. Hewett raced to save his colleague, downing first Slatter then James.

An audience gathered to watch the brawl, which lasted between ten and twelve minutes; a brawl of which the lone constable was inevitably getting the worst. Finally, with help from the crowd and his trusty truncheon, Hewett was able to handcuff Slatter, but James had taken to the hills.

At 5 a.m. on Tuesday 4 April 1899 PC John Charlton passed away, leaving a wife and four young children. Slatter was charged with murder, and incensed police officers searched the area for James. James was finally apprehended thirty-six hours later at Stoke Row by PC Timms. When the pair finally appeared at Reading the charge had been reduced to manslaughter. They were rapidly found guilty, and Justice Day sentenced both men to twenty years' penal servitude.

The victim of the manslaughter at Harwell, PC Charlton (above), and the perpetrators of the crime, Slatter and James (centre). (*Berkshire County Library*)

The romantic Ferry Hotel at Cookham, where Italian Giuseppe Porcolt danced with a pretty barmaid in 1892. Porcolt's amorous advances were interrupted by the raucous tones of the landlord calling for his barmaid to do some work. What could a man of principle do but blast a bullet over the landlord's head? (*Brenda Allaway*)

1942 On this day a slightly less heinous crime was perpetrated at Wokingham. Six evacuee children from London were caught stealing strawberries from Sale & Sons; 4lb of berries had gone missing at *2s 6d* per lb. They were fined *2s 6d* each.

17 June

1915 At Slough petty sessions a fourteen-year-old boy was convicted of stealing a tennis racket worth *10s* from Salthill sports ground. J. Hartopp Nash Esq, chairman of the bench, stated that although this was a shocking and very serious crime he did not intend to send the boy to prison. Instead he would send him somewhere where he would be under good influence and training.

18 June

On the nearest Saturday to this date the good folk of Abingdon give leave to their senses and amid all sorts of inexplicable celebrations the mayor of Ock Street is elected.

19 June

1892 The romantic setting of the picturesque Ferry Hotel at Cookham was shattered by the sound of pistol fire. The ambience of the gently bobbing boats and the calm reflection of the sun on the rippling Thames was split asunder by a fat, red-faced man screaming blue murder and yelling for the police. Only minutes previously serenity had ruled as an attractive dark-skinned Italian named Pelose played an exquisite and faultless Strauss waltz on the hotel's grand piano. There, beside the watching, waving, weeping willows, Pelose's best friend, the even darker and more handsome Giuseppe Porcolt, danced passionately close to an attractive barmaid.

As the maid gazed into the Italian's eyes, harsh words split the air. They came from the hotel's owner, John Billing Kirby, and were to this effect: 'Ain't

Frank Stubbs, a popular baker from Windsor, was killed in a bare-knuckle fight at Virginia Water in 1830. Frank had been felled by a blow in the twenty-first round by a man named Bennett from London. He later expired at the nearby Wheatsheaf public house (right). (*The Wheatsheaf/Brenda Allaway*)

you ever going to do no bleeding work? There are other customers waiting, you know.' Porcolt had to do what a gentleman has to do, when the rapport of his *amore* has been rudely interrupted. Taking a short pistol from his pocket he blasted a bullet 3in above the proprietor's head.

Scene two – Reading Assizes: Outcome: guilty of endangering life and misuse of a firearm six months' hard labour. Did the pretty barmaid wait for Porcolt, one wonders?

20 JUNE **1830** This day brought news of the sad death of Frank Stubbs during a prizefight with a man from London called Bennett. The combatants met at Willington Bridge, Virginia Water, before a vast crowd: the purse was £5. In the twenty-first round Stubbs received a dreadful blow. He was carried to the Wheatsheaf public house where he later died. The *Windsor Gazette* pointed out that this was the third death from prizefighting within a fortnight. Stubbs, a Windsor baker, left a wife and two young children.

21 JUNE **1892** At Reading Assizes Joseph Stark was accused of grievously wounding PC Olley in the town's Silver Street. Numerous witnesses stated that PC Olley had intervened in a serious fracas at Silver Street. It was his intention to arrest Walter Stark, who was behaving violently and had been the instigator of the fight. As the constable grappled with Walter, the latter's brother Joseph stabbed Olley through the lung, an injury that required a seven-week stay in hospital for the constable. Joseph Stark was found guilty and sentenced to six years' penal servitude.

22 JUNE **1929** Alfred Oliver was found by his wife, crumpled in a heap behind the counter of their tobacconist's shop in Cross Street, Reading. Oliver had been smashed over the head with a blunt instrument. Although articulate, on his way to the Royal Berkshire Hospital, at 5.50 p.m. the following day Oliver died of his wounds. Local police were assisted in the investigation by their London counterparts. Certain facts soon became clear: the motive was robbery and the perpetrator was probably local. Witnesses appeared by the dozen; tinkers, local tramps and well-known thieves were called in off the streets.

Although nobody was ever convicted for the murder of Alfred Oliver, there was much national media interest when a well-known actor, Philip Yale Drew, was seized on suspicion. Drew was appearing at Reading Royal Theatre and had been walking in town at the suspected time of the murder. He also fitted the description of a man seen near the tobacconist's by many witnesses. Drew was never taken to court for the offence because the Coroner's Court found the evidence too conflicting. Drew died of cancer of the larynx at Lambeth Hospital in 1940, aged sixty. It is possible he took a dastardly secret to the grave with him. The many and complex twists and turns in this case may be read in an exciting account by Richard Whittington-Egan called *The Ordeal of Philip Yale Drew*.

Alfred Oliver, the murdered Reading tobacconist. *(Berkshire County Library)*

Philip Yale Drew with some of his many supporters. *(Berkshire County Library)*

Wokingham old town hall and the Market Square. It was chock-a-block with military vehicles when an unfortunate young boy was fatally struck by a Jeep in 1944. (*Berkshire County Library*)

23 JUNE **1944** During the Second World War a young boy ran across the Market Square, Wokingham, and was struck by an oncoming Jeep. He died on his way to hospital in a St John ambulance. At the time the Market Square was chock-a-block with military vehicles and servicemen ready to follow the D-Day landings.

24 JUNE **1858** Two ten-year-old boys were committed to Reading gaol for non-payment of fines. The boys were John White and Henry Allaway, who had previously been convicted of throwing stones at an engine driver. The incident occurred between Wokingham and Sandhurst and the driver, who was struck in the mouth, was seriously injured.

25 JUNE **1921** The local media announced the death of Roderick McClean at Broadmoor. McClean was placed in the institution in 1882 after an abortive attempt on the life of Queen Victoria.

26 JUNE **1638** A spell of hot weather brought an increase in the plague that was spreading through Reading. Reputedly starting from a house in Minster Street, the disease spread rapidly through the town. Female searchers were paid well to seek out victims who were taken to the wooden hospital at Whitley Hill. Taxes were levied to pay searchers to remove bodies. Many people kept mastiff dogs as protection against the diseased rats, dogs and hogs that roamed the streets.

27 JUNE **1800** The local media reported that a vast quantity of lead (4cwt) was stolen from Mr Wells's wharf at Maidenhead. A reward of 5 guineas was offered for the apprehension and prosecution of the perpetrator of this atrocious villainy.

1745   At this time it was reported that bribes for the Reading election were expected to be in the region of 30 to 40 guineas. The practice was finally ended by the introduction of secret ballots.

28 June

1893   Local newspapers wrote long articles about the case of Jesse Turner of Sunninghill, who had recently been released from Reading gaol having been found not guilty of manslaughter. Turner had been accused of killing Teddy Graham.

29 June

On 22 March 1893 Teddy Graham, a local odd-job man aged fifty-six, had been drinking all day at the Wells Hotel at Ascot. On being asked to leave, Teddy meandered his way to the New Inn at Sunninghill, where he slept most nights in a broken-down carriage behind the pub. On swaying through the bar entrance Teddy came face to face with the formidable Eleanor Woodham, sister of the landlord. 'You're drunk, Teddy Graham, you'll get no ale here tonight. Go and sleep it off in the carriage.' At the time Jesse Turner, a carpenter and part-time musician, was purchasing some sheet music from local man Fred Jackson. The transaction was interrupted by Teddy Graham: 'You're a fool Jesse Turner, you are being robbed blind, you can get scrap paper at ½*d* a hundredweight anywhere.' Negotiations continued but Teddy would not be denied. 'You're a f—ing fool,' shouted Teddy, his face inches from Jesse's.

The Wells Hotel, Sunninghill. Argumentative drunk Teddy Graham took his last walk from here in 1893.

As a precaution rather than with any intention of injuring the young carpenter, Jesse gave Teddy a shove. The odd-job man staggered towards the door and fell through it. There he lay, his head having struck a concrete stair on the way down. He lay motionless for a few minutes, until several regulars thought it prudent to carry Teddy to his quarters. He was breathing well and even cursing. The following day Teddy died. A Coroner's Court on Friday 24 March indicted Jesse Turner for manslaughter. He was found not guilty in late June after what seemed to be an excessively long time in custody.

30 JUNE **1903** This was the day that strange ghostly shapes or blobs were reported by walkers in Quelm Lane, Warfield. The man-sized apparitions were seen in broad daylight, but they quickly disappeared. Dogs were very reticent to pass the particular spot where they had been seen. The site of the once lovely lane is now part of Quelm Park housing estate. Incidently, quelm is an Old English word for gibbet.

JULY

David Grantham died in 1898. He was one of
Crowthorne's three survivors of the Charge of the
Light Brigade. The last of the three, William Sheppard,
died in July 1900. (*Martin Prescott*)

1 JULY **1905** At Windsor Children's Court three dyed-in-the-wool villains were brought up on the most heinous of crimes. Three eight-year-olds were summoned for unlawfully picking the blooms of a certain tree in the Alexander Gardens, contrary to bylaw 16. Despite pleading not guilty they were fined 1s each.

2 JULY **1937** A Warfield girl was found alive and well on this day. Miss Rose Higgs (aged twenty) had caused much concern when she disappeared from her home seven days previously. Rose's parents and police officers had spent much time trying to locate the young lady. On 2 July a letter was received to say that she had gone into service in Bracknell.

3 JULY **1891** Figures at Maidenhead revealed that one in nineteen of the town's population had appeared before magistrates. There were 8,395 people living in common lodging houses and the tramp population was 12,593. (Such a high figure suggests this is not the population but the number of visits made by tramps to Maidenhead workhouse that year.) In 1890 it is recorded that Maidenhead workhouse received over 1,000 tramps. Why should the figure rise by 11,000 or 12,000 in 12 months?

4 JULY **1937** National and local papers reported on the arrival of Frank Arthur Hart at Broadmoor Asylum. Hart (aged fifty-three), a travelling rep from Ilford, had been found guilty of a double murder at his home in Hillview Crescent. On 28 May suspicious police officers broke into Hart's residence to find the room filled with gas, Hart lying unconscious, and the bodies of his wife and a close female friend, both with horrendous head wounds. At his trial Hart pleaded guilty but insane. He was sentenced to hang. His sentence was later commuted by the Home Secretary to life imprisonment.

5 JULY **1926** On this day a fully clothed young Henley woman was pulled barely alive from the Thames at Wargrave. Her story was terrifyingly strange and mysterious, but unaccountably, not unique. The lady, an attractive, level-headed young woman of education and financial substance, had enjoyed an early evening meal at the George and Dragon. As it was a pleasant evening the lady decided on a riverside stroll. About 200 yards from the inn she heard a low, captivating chanting sound. Looking towards the river she saw the face of what she described as a delightful and mischievous fay or sprite. The face and melodious tone seemed to call her. The urge to hold and possess the young spirit was undeniable and within seconds she found herself

The George and Dragon at Wargrave, where a Henley lady enjoyed a meal before being lured into the Thames by the wicked water spirit, Benji, in 1926. (*Brenda Allaway*)

floundering in the Thames. The two boatmen who rescued the young lady later stated that she had seemed to be mesmerised as she walked into the Thames. The spirit, Benji, is of unknown gender and there have been reports of enticement of both men and women over the years as well as several unaccountable suicides near the spot. The only untimely death in the vicinity was that of a ferryman's young daughter in 1879 (see 25 January).

1585 This is reputed to be the day when John Greenwoode was pressed to death at Reading for refusing to plead guilty or not guilty. It is not known of what crime Greenwoode was originally accused, but as pleading not guilty

6 JULY

John Greenwoode had a pressing engagement at Reading. This scene, actually from Newgate, shows gaolers hoping to extract a plea. If a suspect refused to plead he could save his estate from going to the Crown after his death.

and then being found guilty resulted not only in the usual death sentence but also one's land being forfeited to the state, many brave men chose not to plead, thereby enduring a torturous death, in order to save their estates for their families. There were various methods of pressing a prisoner to death; one of the most common was to place larger and larger rocks on the accused's chest.

7 July

1896 Trooper Charles Woolridge walked to his death at Reading gaol. The famous hangman, Billington, who despatched him, stated that the young soldier went to his death with great courage.

In early 1896 Charles T. Woolridge, a trooper of ten years, was living in a separate abode to his wife Laura, he in London and she with friends at Arthur Road, Clewer, Windsor. Their relationship had long been strained. Woolridge had a white-hot temper and this, coupled with a suspicion that his wife was not entirely faithful, often led to violent confrontations. On 16 March Woolridge called on Laura at Clewer; within minutes a row broke out in which the trooper struck his wife repeatedly in the face. When he left Laura sported two black eyes and was badly bloodied at nose and mouth. On returning to his quarters Woolridge wrote his wife a letter, declaring his undying love, but, realising they could not live in harmony, he said it would be best if they never met again. If only Woolridge had kept to his word.

On 29 March at 9 p.m. the trooper once again called on his wife. Within seconds Alice Cox, who lived with Laura, heard two screams coming from near the front door. On investigation she found Laura lying dead. Her throat had been viciously cut. At 9.20 p.m. Woolridge walked into Windsor police station and blandly stated: 'I have killed my wife. I have slit her throat.'

Oscar Wilde told the tale of trooper Charles T. Woolridge in his *Ballad of Reading Gaol*. *(Illustrated London News)*

He was taken into custody and at his subsequent trial Charles T. Woolridge was found guilty of murder and sentenced to death. While Woolridge was awaiting his execution, one of his co-prisoners was Oscar Wilde, who was serving a term for homosexual practices. Wilde described Woolridge's death in his *Ballad of Reading Gaol*:

> Yet each man kills the thing he loves,
> By each let this be heard,
> Some do it with a bitter look.
> Some with a flattering word.
> The coward does it with a kiss,
> The brave man with a sword!

The man's death was immortalised in verse, but his name is virtually unknown.

1951 On 13 July the *Windsor Express* stated: 'Windsor was shocked and grieved this weekend by the disappearance of 7½-year-old Christine Butcher, who lived with her parents and elder brother in a flat at 138 Peascod Street Windsor.' Christine's body had been found on the 10th, having disappeared on the 8th. The *Express* went on to say: 'The worst fears were confirmed when late on Tuesday evening the ravished body of the little girl was discovered in Home Park. She had been strangled by the belt of the Macintosh she had been wearing.' Professor Keith Simpson was called in, as was Superintendent George Salter of Scotland Yard. The case was a difficult one. It is described in fuller detail in Simpson's *Forty Years of Murder*. Not the least of the detectives' problems was the number of people who used the park – the home of the Royal Shows. Also at this particular time Sugar Ray Robinson was training nearby and, as always, the boxer was attended by a massive entourage, adding to the number of people the police had to interview. Christine Butcher's brutal slayer was never found. It remains one of the saddest and most emotive of crimes.

The grave of Christine Butcher. (*By kind permission of Arthur Spicer*)

1883 At Windsor petty sessions Richard Harding of Windsor was charged with assaulting his wife by tweaking her nose and causing it to bleed copiously. Harding said he had been drunk for a week and could remember nothing. 'Are you sober now?' enquired Mr Long, chairman of the bench. 'I believe so Sir,' came the reply. Harding was warned of dire consequences if he appeared again and was then let off with a caution.

1883 At Windsor petty sessions Florrie Proudlock, a young woman of twenty, was charged with being drunk and disorderly in Victoria Street. She was remanded until the 12th. On that occasion Miss Proudlock said she was disgusted with herself and should she be released she would return to her husband in London. Asked by Mr Long if she knew where to find her husband, Florrie replied that she had sent word for him to meet her at the Ship and Bottle, Southwark. She was dismissed with a caution.

On 11 July 1672 Margaret Adams was ordered to be ducked. It is not known of what she was suspected, but it was almost certainly associated with witchcraft.

11 JULY   **1672**   On this day Margaret Adams of Newbury was ordered to be ducked, but her misdemeanour remains unknown.

12 JULY   **1883**   At Windsor petty sessions, Mary Anne Ducket of Garden Court, Windsor, was charged before the bench with using obscene language. The charge was denied but after the court heard many witnesses Ducket was convicted and fined £2, with one month's imprisonment in default.

13 JULY   **1834**   At the Berkshire Assizes William Powell, William Winchcombe and Mary Anne Towers were charged with stealing two gowns, two shawls and two dresses, the property of Jonathan Towers, father to one of the accused. It transpired in court that Jonathan Towers had banished his daughter from his home in Winkfield for associating with undesirable people. On returning home from business in early March he discovered that glass had been removed from a bedroom window and that the above items were missing. He immediately contacted the authorities. Constable Edwards deposed in court that, acting on information received, he and Constable Denby approached the White Hart at Egham. There they arrested all three of the accused and also found the above-mentioned clothing in a bedroom that had been rented by Mary Anne Towers. Powell and Winchcombe were found guilty and each sentenced to six months' hard labour. Mary Anne Towers was found not guilty.

14 JULY   **1787**   At Abingdon quarter sessions for stealing bacon from a house at Speenhamland Richard Thomas was sentenced to be whipped and to serve three months of hard labour; William Brant, for stealing five pigs, was to be whipped this day and the same day of each month while serving three months of hard labour; Thomas Pace, for leaving his family, was to receive three months' hard labour; John Allen, for an assault on John Appleton, was sentenced to one month in a closed cell of solitary confinement and was fined 11*s*. William Watts, Henry Ghost, James Peaty, Christopher Lawrence and James Heiford, all of Wokingham, were convicted of assaulting and beating William Taplin, a surgeon of that town. It transpired that the men suspected Taplin of writing an article against bullbaiting, an exhibition for which Wokingham was famous. All received long prison sentences.

1817 A Reading paper reported that Thomas Ayres was hanged for housebreaking with violence at Sulhampstead Abbots. Mr Ayres will have to remain an enigma recorded in one paragraph of a local paper.   15 JULY

1841 John Dormer was hanged at Reading on this day. Dormer, aged nineteen, left his new wife and set off to Portsmouth to join the Navy. This ambition he achieved but the long hours and hard work did not suit him. When he returned to Portsmouth he jumped ship and headed for the hills, the Chiltern Hills at High Wycombe, where his young wife was still living. He was now officially a deserter, which complicated his life. It meant lodging with friends and only getting the most arduous of labouring jobs. It was not long before Dormer was breaking into houses and shops to subsidise his precarious existence and, as often happens in these situations, Dormer fell in with men of his own ilk. His special colleague was one Richard Alder of Marlow. Alder was of similar age to Dormer but of a quite well-to-do and wealthy family. While robbery was a necessity to Dormer, to Alder it was an adventurous pastime.   16 JULY

Early in July 1801 the pair set about robbing a stagecoach on the Bath Road near Cookham. They selected a bend in the road, armed themselves with pistols, then lay in wait. It was not a successful enterprise. Alder had thought that the coaches would slow down for the bend. This they did, but on seeing Dormer and Alder they set off again at a cracking pace. After three failed attempts the duo gave up in despair. Then fate played a hand in the shape of a farmer named Robinson. As he was snoozing his way home in his horse and cart he was surprised by two men aiming pistols at him. Each had his face covered by a cravat. Robinson was not the man to give up his hard-earned money easily. As he got down from his cart to confront them he was struck in the temple by a shot from the young man's pistol. Within a minute he lay dead.

The following day Alder and Dormer were arrested; they had been heard planning the stage robbery in the local Fleece Inn. The police knew that they had the right men but the evidence was circumstantial. Harsh interviews followed; Dormer resisted rudely but Alder was more amiable. He told the police that he thought they were flagging the farmer down for a lift; he could not have been more surprised when Dormer fetched out a pistol and shot the poor man. Dormer was charged with murder and Alder was released, although he freely admitted afterwards it was he who had fired the shot. A dejected John Dormer was hanged at Reading gaol. His body was then publicly dissected by surgeons in Reading town hall.

17 July **1581** On this day Edmund Campion was taken prisoner at Lyford Grange near Wantage. Campion, a brilliant man, had been one of Queen's Elizabeth's favourites. However, his life seemed fated after he converted to Roman Catholicism and his departure for the Jesuit Seminary at Douai, France, did not help his popularity. However, it was suicidal to return to England to lecture to his fellow Catholics. Campion arrived secretly at Dover in June 1580 and was smuggled into Camberwell. Here he was betrayed by a man named Pounde and once had to flee to rural Berkshire. His final indiscretion was to place a pamphlet, giving ten good reasons why the Anglican Church was not a valid church on every pew in St Mary's Church, Oxford. Now under an arrest warrant, Campion stayed with his friend Yates at Lyford. He was once again betrayed, this time by a man named Eliot. The house was searched and Campion arrested and lodged in the Tower. Having been stretched on the rack Campion was strangely able to have a debate with the Dean of Windsor, after which he was taken to Tyburn on a hurdle and hanged.

18 July **1910** This was the day that William Broome, a young man from Oxford Street, Reading, was charged with the horrendous murder of seventy-year-old Isabella Wilson, who kept a second-hand shop in the High Street, Slough. She had been tied up, then beaten and tortured as her assailant attempted to find her nest egg – an attempt that was – apparently successful. Broome was soon arrested and half a dozen witnesses put him

Slough High Street, where William Broome beat and tortured seventy-year-old Isabella Wilson to death in 1910. *(Berkshire County Library)*

at the scene. He also had a scratched face, and bloodstains found on his boots were of the same group as Mrs Wilson's. His ridiculous alibi fell apart, partially aided by a disillusioned girlfriend. The media made little of the case, probably because it coincided with the trial of Dr Crippen, which was front-page news with all the nationals. Broome was found guilty and sentenced to hang on 16 November at Reading. He appealed against his conviction but this only postponed the inevitable. He was eventually hanged at Pentonville on 23 November.

1907   On this day at Clewer, William Austin, alias Saunder, was charged with the murder of Unity Butler. On 16 July the thirteen-year-old's body was found in the bedroom of her mother's lodger, William Austin. She had been bound, gagged, raped and finally strangled. Austin, who was also a cousin to Mrs Butler, was suspected from the first. Before the murder was discovered he took off on his bicycle. Austin was arrested on 17 July by Sergeant Tanzer. He was found on the sparsely populated Winkfield Plain where he had spent the night. At his trial Austin stated that he was lying on his bed when Unity came in and started to tease him. He then tied her up to get some peace. Things got out of hand and he strangled her. His plea for insanity being turned down, Austin was hanged at Reading on 5 November.

The bound, gagged and raped body of thirteen-year-old Unity Butler was found in Arthur Road, Clewer, in 1907. The prime suspect, her mother's cousin, William Austin, disappeared on his bicycle. *(Brenda Allaway)*

1847   Vivien Teyrell, described as a champion from Henley, was fined £1 at Wokingham Court for an assault on Charles Bradshaw Sharpe. It appears there was a brawl in a Wokingham tavern where Teyrell broke a chair across Sharpe's head.

1857   The *Reading Mercury* and many of its readers were shocked by the sentence passed on one Charles Appleton. The report stated that 'considerable astonishment in court was shown over the light sentence'. On 21 June an argument broke out at Kings Meadow, Reading, between two teams that were mowing. The team led by a man named Lawrence was working on privately owned ground and doing a far better job than the Reading Council team, run by a man named Fuller. Insults were exchanged before Charles Appleton of Fuller's team ran up behind Lawrence and struck him a blow, which resulted in Lawrence's death. In mid-July at Reading Court Appleton was found guilty of manslaughter and sentenced to three weeks in prison. The public found this astonishing – at the time seven years' transportation was not uncommon as the penalty for stealing a pocket handkerchief.

22 JULY **1839** It was reported that four prisoners had escaped from Reading gaol. The men were being kept in the condemned cell awaiting transfer to Abingdon. Their means of escape involved removing a loose lintel and forcing a window.

23 JULY **1537** This is reputed to be the day that a Wallingford man was placed in the pillory after having his ears cut off. His crime was to spread a rumour that Henry VIII was dead.

24 JULY **1913** A haunting was reported at the George Hotel in Reading. The spirit, witnessed on five or six occasions, was that of a housemaid. Local papers featured the story after sightings on consecutive nights. The apparition disappeared as quickly as it had arrived, and no sightings have been reported since.

> **SHOCKING CASE OF MANSLAUGHTER IN THE KING'S MEADOW.**
>
> On Thursday evening, between seven and eight o'clock, much excitement was created by a report that a man had been killed in the King's meadow, and soon afterwards the capture of the perpetrator of the dreadful act, accompanied by a large crowd of persons, to the police station, confirmed the sad story. In ordinary cases, where any doubt is entertained, and the defence of a prisoner may be affected by the publication of details, or observations may prejudice the case, we should exercise much care, even at the expense of withholding information. But here the facts are so clear and simple, and so fully borne out by the evidence, that we cannot hesitate to place them before the public.
>
> It appears, that at the time of this tragical occurrence there were two parties of men engaged mowing in the King's meadow, which, as most of our readers know, is situated just north of the railway, between it and the river Thames, and is the spot on which Reading races are held. One of the parties was in the employ of Mr. G. Shackel, of Early Court, who rents a small portion of the meadow, the other by persons who bought the grass at the recent public sale. Some dispute arose between a man named Case and Mr. Shackel's foreman, Joseph Lawrance, as to a few yards of grass. Appleton also interfered, and was urged on to violence by Case and another man named Holmes. Eventually Lawrance, who was a particularly civil and respectable man, declined the challenge of Appleton, observing that he was maimed of three fingers, and was walking away, when Appleton rushed after him, and struck him two violent blows at the base of the skull, or just on the neck, behind. The poor fellow staggered, threw up his hands, his eyes glared with agony, he fell forward, and what one minute before was a form in the vigour of life and manhood was a senseless corpse.
>
> Just before this Mr. Shackel had come on the ground, and at the risk of personal violence from Appleton and his confederates, had interfered. He saw his faithful servant thus cruelly slaughtered, and went off for medical aid, but this was unavailing. We subjoin the details from the evidence given before the magistrates.
>
> Yesterday before the Mayor, E. Purvis, and T. Morris, Esqrs., William Appleton was placed at the bar, charged with feloniously killing one Joseph Lawrance, and Richard Case and George Holmes with being concerned in the killing of Joseph Lawrance.

25 JULY **1900** On this day it was announced that Crowthorne had lost its third and last survivor of the Charge of the Light Brigade. The befuddled orders at Balaklava cost the lives of more than half of the regiment. The village of Crowthorne was unique in having three local survivors. The three that returned from the ill-advised charge and subsequent slaughter on 25 October 1854 were, firstly, Amos Hallet, David Grantham and William Sheppard. Hallet lived in the village for many years. He died in 1890 and is buried in the churchyard there. Grantham, who died in 1898 at Owlsmoor, aged sixty-seven, was given a full military funeral, with details from over a dozen regiments attending, led by the band of Sandhurst Royal Military College. His medals were carried behind the coffin, which was draped with the Union flag. After retiring from the Services Grantham took over the White Swan at Sandhurst. The third local hero of Balaklava was William Sheppard, who had enlisted in 1853 by lying about his age – he was actually only fifteen years old. He was severely wounded at Balaklava and became a Russian prisoner. Repatriated, he was discharged from the services as unfit.

The *Reading Mercury* was concerned about the light sentence (three weeks) handed down to Charles Appleton for the manslaughter of a man named Lawrence at Kings Meadow in 1857.

GALLANTRY AT SANDHURST
Warden Decorated For Brave Action

Two Sandhurst people—one a warden—have received the British Empire Medal for their part in a gallant effort to rescue the crew of a R.A.F. aircraft which had crashed and burst into flames. Other residents have been commended for their conduct.

Those decorated are Mr. Frederick Harry Smith, a 67 years old warden who has been in the service for five and a quarter years and lives at West Ridge, and Mr. William Henry May, of New Road, Sandhurst. Commended for their bravery, are Mr. Leonard Arthur Williams, of Fox Inn, Mr. Francis Peabody, of 4 Searle Street, Bracknell; Mrs. Mabel Goswell, of 1 Rose Cottages, Longsdown Road, Little Sandhurst; Mrs. Eva Butters, of Woodstock, Longdon Road, Sandhurst; Mr. Leveson William Goswell, of Heatherside, Longsdown Road, Little Sandhurst.

An Air Ministry bulletin says that when a Boston aircraft crashed and burst into flames at Sandhurst in January Smith and Aircraftman S. Rance who was on leave at Sandhurst, ran to help although the 'plane was blazing so intensely that from the first rescue seemed hopeless. The

Sydney Rance, the hero of Sandhurst, was posthumously mentioned in dispatches on 26 July 1944. His house is on the right in this picture of Little Sandhurst. *(Tony Rance)*

Unfortunately Sheppard was too young and hadn't done enough service to be granted a pension. Although severely handicapped by crutches, Sheppard managed to marry three different women and have sixteen children.

1944 This day brought the posthumous mention in dispatches of A/C Sydney Rance RAF. Rance, who was home on leave, rushed to assist when a RAF bomber crashed into the grounds of Eagle House School, Sandhurst. Rance was trying desperately to open the door when the bombs on board exploded. The 41-year-old left a wife and baby son at Little Sandhurst.

26 JULY

1880 Very few people have heard of the Battle of Maiwand, which was fought in Afghanistan. Although it has only been fleetingly referred to in history books it had great significance in Berkshire. The British Army was routed by Afghan troops, leaving the Royal Berkshire Regiment to cover their retreat. Over 300 Berkshire men died in one day. They are commemorated by the Great Lion that stands in Reading's Forbury Gardens.

27 JULY

The famous Forbury lion. It commemorates the 300 Berkshire men who perished at the little-known Battle of Maiwand in 1880. *(Brenda Allaway)*

28 JULY   **1787** The news was announced that well-known villain Thomas Ryder had broken out of the dungeon at Marlow in which he had been confined. Ryder was being kept on suspicion of robbing a house at Birchetts Green, near Maidenhead. He had recently returned from the *Ballast Lighters* (a floating prison ship), where he had been confined for three years for robbing a house at Hurley. Ryder was described as short, dark-complexioned and wearing a blue frock coat and waistcoat.

29 JULY   **1908** It was reported that Mr Weedon, the County Coroner, was worried about the number of deaths at Broadmoor Asylum. The previous ten days had seen the demise of Mary Ann Maddock (fifty-two), who had murdered her infant daughter in Derby in 1879 (heart disease); Henry Brady (seventy-five), a shipwright, committed to Broadmoor for burglary (congestion of the brain and epilepsy); George Stratton (fifty), a dangerous lunatic who murdered a woman in Chelmsford in 1882 (pyelitis); John Exler (seventy-six), a man of independent means (asthma and heart disease); and finally, James Forbes (fifty-seven), convicted in 1904 of damaging a Hackney carriage (cancer).

30 JULY   **1891** At Newbury petty sessions Charles Henwood was charged with stealing an umbrella and being drunk and disorderly at Newbury. He was sentenced to seven days' hard labour. Charles Warman, charged with being drunk and disorderly at Hampstead Norris, also received seven days' hard labour. Finally, Charles Gardner was sent to the quarter sessions for stealing a watch at Hungerford. Three proper Charlies!

31 JULY   **1808** Three men accused of poaching on the Runnymede estate were named as Silas Bell, Elisha Book and Jasper Candell. Each received fines with imprisonment in default.

AUGUST

Miss Blandy in her cell at Oxford Prison. She had killed
her father, but escaped from house arrest in Henley to the
Little Angel Inn in Berkshire in August 1751.
(*Berkshire County Library*)

Hurst church, the final resting place of Herbert Baigent. He was murdered by a fellow worker at Hurst Lodge. *(Brenda Allaway)*

1 AUGUST

1891 This was the date when a murder took place in the peaceful village of St Nicholas, Hurst. Two of Major General Beauchamp's staff at Hurst Lodge were at odds with each other. One of them, Herbert Baigent, had been with the major for four years, since leaving school. At the time of his demise he was just nineteen. William Lazell had recently been employed as a coachman and lived in one of the farm cottages with his wife and eleven-year-old child.

The pair did not get on generally, owing to many niggling irritations. There was, to put it bluntly, a clash of personalities. The situation was not helped when Herbert ordered Lazell's son from the orchard where he was trying to dislodge apples. The following morning Lazell decided to have a word with Baigent while he was milking the cows. The ensuing argument soon became heated and culminated with Lazell smashing Baigent's skull with a fork, killing him instantly. Apparently not satisfied, Lazell continued to stab and beat the deceased man. Finally the coachman came to his senses and realised what he had done. William Lazell was arrested and lodged at Wokingham police station. The next day at Wokingham Magistrates Court he was charged with the wilful murder of Herbert Baigent. Committed to the assizes, Lazell was lodged at Reading Gaol.

On 11 November William Lazell stated that he admitted striking the blow but had no intention of killing Baigent. After a little over two hours the jury reached a guilty verdict. It was followed by a plea for clemency on account of Lazell's previous good character. However, the death sentence was pronounced. A total of 5,900 people signed a petition and the Secretary of State advised Her Majesty Queen Victoria to commute the sentence to one of penal servitude for life; on 20 November 1891 the appeal was granted.

2 AUGUST

1817 James Castle was hanged at Reading on this day. On 21 July that year the Castle gang was apprehended at Abingdon. The Castle brothers, James and Henry, had surrounded themselves with the most disreputable gang of blackguards and felons ever to congregate in the county. Rustling was their main pastime and they were thought to be responsible for over 200 missing sheep each year. James, Henry and two lieutenants were caught red-handed with seven purloined sheep at an Abingdon barn. The four were 'persuaded' to inform on a dozen others. The judge at the quarter sessions handed out long terms of imprisonment and transportation. James and Henry were sentenced to hang. At the eleventh hour, Henry, the younger brother, was reprieved and transported to Australia. James was hanged; the *Mercury* reported that he went to his death 'With firm step and utter resignation'.

1976 At a Coroner's Court it was decided that James Charles Young, aged twenty-five, of Leyton, had died from natural causes. Young, a commercial clerk, had suffered an epileptic fit while swimming in the Thames at Bourne End. Witnesses stated that during the fit James had disappeared under the water. Despite repeated efforts from his brother and two friends James could not be found. His body surfaced some three hours later.

3 AUGUST

1833 The details of the offences of three men hanged at Reading on this day seem remarkably unreported. One would have thought that three men meeting their maker on the same day would have evoked considerable excitement. The record states only that Edward Green, Thomas Lincoln and James Morris were hanged at Reading for burglary.

4 AUGUST

1831 On this day two underwrappers, Smith and Papps, working at the Star and Garter at Windsor, were charged with cutting the harnesses of several gentlemen's horses. Found guilty, they were fined *2s* each plus costs, with six months' imprisonment in default of payment. Cutting a harness, usually part-way through, was extremely dangerous and was often a result of the stable hands deciding that they had not been paid enough.

5 AUGUST

Don't leave your horse at the Star and Garter, Windsor! In 1831 two under-wrappers were found guilty of cutting harnesses. (*Brenda Allaway*)

6 August   **1831**   On this day the good folks of Bisham were surprised to see a tall respectable-looking man, well dressed and wearing a top hat, strolling along a path by the Thames. There was nothing strange about the man, only his companion – a spotted boy. The boy, black and pink mottled, was less than five years old. His skin was as unsightly as it was unique. In all probability he suffered from the skin disease ichthyosis serpentina that causes terrible scaly blotches all over the body. The man was the impresario John Richardson of Marlow. He had risen from a workhouse boy to become a national showman specialising in freaks. At the height of his popularity Richardson had performed before Queen Victoria at Windsor. Of all his freaks Richardson is thought to have had a special affection for the boy, whom he named George Alexander Gratton. He claimed that he had found him in the West Indies and saved him from a life of poverty and ill treatment. Although a showman to the end, it is reported that Richardson was genuinely heartbroken when the 'Spotted Boy' died at Marlow, aged just five.

The good citizens of Bisham were rather surprised in August 1831 to see a well-dressed man and a black-and-pink spotted boy strolling beside the Thames. (Brenda Allaway)

7 August   **1819**   Two young men, Edward Tooley, aged nineteen, and David Pattence, aged twenty-five, were hanged at Reading on this date. In late July at 2 a.m., three men had broken into the house of Thomas Smith at Langford. Smith, a middle-aged businessman, lived alone, save for a housemaid who had a bedroom at the other end of the house. The intruders set about Smith with fence posts until the deceased had breathed his last. They then ransacked the house, stealing silver and banknotes, before fading into the night, after checking the housemaid who was feigning sleep. In a small village it was not long before three local lads were arrested. Their downfall was their unusually lavish spending. Unbeknown to them Smith had survived, although in a terrible condition. The housemaid, who had lain there terrified, had heard the accused using Christian names. It would have been thought that the local authorities had sufficient evidence for a guilty verdict, but for some reason they persuaded one of the three, John Hall, to turn King's evidence. This he did with relish, stating that he was only the lookout and did not come inside the house. Ultimately Hall walked free, while Tooley and Pattence went to meet their maker.

8 August   **1751**   This is the day that Mary Blandy, who was under house arrest at Henley while her father's death was being investigated, made a dash for freedom. Probably spurred on by the abuse hurled at her and the threats of violence, Mary ran across the bridge to the Little Angel Inn on the Berkshire side. Here she was surrounded by irate and screaming townsfolk. Mary was collected by the town sergeant, Richard Fisher, and escorted back to her home. She stayed there but briefly. The authorities finding a case of murder transported Mary to Oxford Prison. At Oxford Assizes Mary was found guilty of the murder of her father. She killed him because he did not approve of her beau, Captain Willy Cranstow, who had fled to France. Mary Blandy, spinster of Henley, committer of patricide, victim of infatuation, mounted the gallows at Oxford on 6 April 1752.

1850 On this day an apparition was witnessed by several people in the Faringdon churchyard. It was said to be the terrifying spectre of the headless ghost of Hampden Pye. A native of Faringdon, Pye was an officer in the eighteenth-century Royal Navy. His stepmother is reputed to have bribed his captain to have his head blown off in a naval engagement. After his 'accidental demise' Pye's ghost sought revenge on those responsible for his 'condition'. His headless spectre appeared in his stepmother's coach, in the captain's cabin and also at the home of the gunner. Pye's ghost seems to have settled in Faringdon churchyard where it makes the occasional guest appearance.

9 AUGUST

1728 This is reputed to be the day that Sir William East bought Hall Place at Burchetts Green. Sir William is said to have built the present mansion. In Nelson's field, trees were planted to show the formation of Nelson's ships at Trafalgar. Hall Place adjoins Maidenhead Thicket, a notorious place for highwaymen. Claude Duval, one of the most famous, is said to haunt the hall's grounds, as well as a group of Druids, a ghostly coach and horses and a black servant.

10 AUGUST

1914 The first German prisoners of war are reputed to have arrived at Broadmoor on this date. They had originally been housed at the military prison hospital at Netley, near Southampton. A tongue-in-cheek question asked at the time was: 'Are all German soldiers deemed to be mentally ill and dangerous?'

11 AUGUST

1733 This was one of the days that Beenham Vallence was having trouble with its scandalous vicar. The Revd Thomas Stackhouse, who was author of *History of the Bible*, was a genius and a drunkard. Stackhouse wrote most of his famous history at a hut called Jack's Booth, near what is now the A4. He obviously suffered from what was called 'alcoholic melancholy' (depression). During his

12 AUGUST

The ghost of Hampden Pye of Faringdon sat in his stepmother's coach, haunted the gunner who blew his head off, and, as seen here, the captain of his ship. *(From an engraving by John Leech)*

Beenham's brilliant but scandalous vicar, Jack Stackhouse, spent much of his life in a drunken stupor at Jack's Booth, later to become the Three Kings, Mulligan's and finally the Spring Inn. (*Brenda Allaway*)

sermons at church on a Sunday, Stackhouse would break into incoherent prayers and then burst into tears. He would then beg for forgiveness and vow to mend his ways. Jack's Booth became a pub named the Three Kings. After many metamorphoses into fish restaurants and other businesses, it is now an inn again.

13 August **1834** William Wilson and James Warwick were charged with beating and robbing a young man named Evans near the Long Walk at Windsor Castle. Evans deposed that he was entering the Walk on Saturday night, when Wilson seized him by the collar and then threw him to the ground. While Wilson held him face down, Warwick relieved him of his hat, gloves, pocket-handkerchief and 17s 10d in change. Warwick was attempting to remove his boots when his cries of 'murder' brought assistance and the pair fled. Next evening the two men were arrested at the Union public house in Windsor, where they were rolling drunk. Warwick, who had Evans's hat on over his cap, was in possession of 4s in silver, and Wilson had 4d in copper. Both men were despatched to Reading where they were to be held in custody until the quarter sessions. Frustratingly, there is no record of the outcome of this case.

14 August **1769** This was the birthday of Richard, 7th Earl of Barrymore. Barrymore came to Wargrave as a boy and returned after an education at Eton. His family was extremely wealthy, and this permitted Barrymore to indulge in riotous behaviour. Wargrave was inflicted with the lord and his brothers. They would steal coaches and horses and drive them through the village at breakneck speed, smashing windows with their whips and firing at inn signs. By the age of eighteen Barrymore had earned the nickname 'Hellgate', and his capacity for gambling and spending was enormous. He would wager on anything, however absurd, and even bet the Duke of Bedford that he could find someone to eat a live cat.

Apart from his hooliganism and vandalism Barrymore was quite a substantial asset to the village of Wargrave. He initiated sports and gave generously to the poor. He also built a theatre at his home, Barrymore House, which stands by the side of the Thames. Unfortunately the money began to run out and, as debtors gathered, Barrymore absconded – accompanied by a Miss Goulding. Finally Barrymore joined the Berkshire Militia, but while escorting French prisoners in 1793 his carelessly placed gun went off, shooting him dead. Barrymore House still stands by the Thames but Lord Barrymore's debtors pulled down his theatre in 1792. The stones were auctioned to pay off his outstanding debts.

1883   At Maidenhead Borough Court Walter Smith of Staines was charged with obstructing William Turner, a lock-keeper, in the execution of his duty. A local paper stated that Smith, who had already done battle with boathooks, attacking other river users, proceeded to push Turner from his position near the wheel and attempted to open the lock-gates. Back in court Smith defended his action by stating that he was going upriver but had been waiting at Boulter's Lock for 2½ hours while Turner had kept the gates closed. He apologised for his actions that were born of frustration.   **15 August**

1867   William Carter, a countryman, took a trip into nearby Newbury. He bought some corduroy trousers at Burges's shop and various small items from other establishments; his shopping expedition being punctuated by   **16 August**

On 13 August 1834 William Wilson and James Warwick were charged with beating and robbing a young man called Evans near the Long Walk. Below motor cars are parked in the Long Walk for a royal garden party, 1908. (*Michael Stiles*)

Wargrave High Street. Little has changed since Richard, Lord 'Hellgate' Barrymore, rode the streets putting bullets through the signs of local inns. (*Brenda Allaway*)

regular calls at the Globe, the Royal Exchange and other places of refreshment. Leaving between 11 and 12 p.m., Carter made his way along Wash Road towards his home. As he walked a young lady, who stopped and chatted, overtook him. After she had gone Carter discovered that his new trousers and groceries were missing. He chased after the girl but failed to catch her. Carter then made his way back to Newbury and awoke a policeman.

The following day, aided by Carter's description, Sergeant Hinds made his way to a boarding house owned by one Mark Tuck. There he interviewed a young woman named Elizabeth Shefford. In her room he found jars of pickle, similar to those lost by Carter, and a pair of corduroy trousers hanging on the

On a hot summer day at Boulter's Lock tempers frayed and Walter Smith of Staines lost patience and pushed the lock-keeper from his place at the wheel. (*Author's Collection*)

outside fence. The accused was arrested and taken into custody, where Carter later identified her. At Reading quarter sessions Shefford was sentenced to six months' imprisonment.

1916 At Maidenhead Borough Court a very smart young lady, Florence 'Nelly' Groves, was charged with being drunk and disorderly. PC Miles stated that on the previous Saturday night at 9.55 p.m. he had been patrolling central Maidenhead when he noticed a crowd of women outside the Queen's Arms. On pushing his way through he had found Nelly fast asleep, with her clothes in disarray, cuddling a Canadian soldier who seemed to be in much the same condition. PC Miles shook Nelly lightly, whereupon she declared: 'How dare you come into my bedroom and molest me.' Miles pointed out that they were not in her bedroom and arrested her. She was found guilty and fined 10s. Joe King, the Canadian soldier, was discharged to the Canadian military authorities.

17 August

1891 At Newbury petty sessions Alfred Ludgrove was charged with trespass at Hampstead Norris. The gamekeeper's apprentice John Wilson stated that he had heard a shot and gone to investigate. He had found Ludgrove and accused him of poaching. Ludgrove asked Wilson: 'If I was poaching where are the rabbits?' 'You probably missed,' replied Wilson. 'I have never missed in my life,' stated the other. As no evidence could be found the charge was altered to the lesser one of trespass. Found guilty, Ludgrove was fined 15s with seven days' imprisonment in default.

18 August

1936 Two boys, aged fourteen, who seemed to be excessively drunk, lay across the railway line near Wokingham station. The boys from Little Sandhurst were kept in Wokingham lock-up for twenty-four hours and then released with a stern warning.

19 August

1936 This was one of those days when motorists on the A338, near Hungerford, were surprised by the appearance of a phantom horsewoman. The woman, astride a white horse, leapt across the road in front of oncoming cars, causing them to brake sharply. By the time the shaken motorists opened their windows to complain, both horse and rider had disappeared.

20 August

1867 At Newbury petty sessions John Ludgrove, an elderly man with a long history of fraud, was charged with dishonestly obtaining 1s. John Wilmot of Crookham came into Newbury on market day, his donkey and cart loaded with vegetables to sell, and set up at the Weavers Arms. Realising that he had an order for two bushels of grain that he had inadvertently left at home, and scared of losing an important customer, Wilmot sought to rectify the situation by approaching John Ludgrove. Handing him 1s Wilmot instructed him to rush down to Hawkins and Canning and bring him back two bushels of grain. This way he would make no profit but he would keep a valued customer. The customer came and went; Ludgrove went but didn't come.

21 August

After four hours Wilmot reported his loss to a constable. In court Ludgrove admitted the offence and stated that he had drunk the money. He was sentenced to one month in gaol.

22 August **1891** Arthur Vardy of Southampton was charged with driving a locomotive through the town of Newbury during prohibited hours. Vardy was stopped in Northbrook Street at 4 p.m. by PC Gibbs. In court Vardy said he had asked several people on the outskirts of the town and they had informed him that there was no ban on motorised vehicles at the time. He was fined 10s.

23 August **1891** This was the day that Frederick William Gibson was summoned at Newbury for letting a cow stray onto the main thoroughfare. Gibson stated that he hired a field at Eastfields from the Lord of the Manor and it was the owner's responsibility to keep the gates and fence in order. He had hired a boy at 10s a week to watch the gate until the owner shouldered his responsibility. The boy had obviously not been doing his appointed task. Mr Gibson was let off with a caution.

24 August **1883** On this day the *Maidenhead Advertiser* published a letter in its column 'The Looker On'. The letter criticised a 'Mad Dog' that had been executed publicly for biting several people. It stated that the dog did not have rabies as first thought, but owed its rebellious nature to being chained up for days on end in extreme heat. Temperatures ranged from 80° to 90°F. When the poor creature finally escaped it was chased by a group of men brandishing sticks. The writer deemed it to be 'Small wonder that the poor creature, when cornered, turned and bit someone'.

25 August **1315** On or about this date there was a furious row going on between the Vachel family, which had owned much of Reading since the thirteenth century, and the Abbot of Reading Abbey. The bone of contention was the use of a pathway that crossed John Vachel's land at Great Coley Park. The path, which meandered over a stone bridge spanning the River Holybrook, had been used by the Reading monks for a century. The monks looked upon the crossing as their god-given right. Vachel did not and prohibited its use. To prove his point, the infuriated Abbot sent a monk with a wagonload of corn across the bridge. To prove his point, Vachel put the monk to the sword, killing him instantly. He then proceeded to tip the cart and its contents into the river. The Abbot's reaction was to excommunicate Vachel and then heavily fine him before he could gain absolution. Not too drastic a sentence one might think, at a time when peasants were hanged for stealing a loaf of bread. As a further penance Vachel was forced to change his family's motto to ''tis better to suffer than to revenge'.

26 August **1793** The official opening day of Reading County Gaol. John Howard, the famous prison reformer, had condemned Old Castle Street Prison, which housed both men and women. The old prison had a treadmill that could be watched by the public; it was quite an attraction.

1913 On this day local papers reported on a sighting of the Phantom Maid of the Olde Rose Inn at Wokingham. The rather embroidered story tells of a maid in the 1760s who found herself pregnant by a commercial traveller. He promised to return but never did (much to the maid's surprise). There was only one honourable thing to do; she hanged herself in the kitchen. Her ghost was witnessed regularly in the back downstairs bar with a mournful look upon her face. Three fires at the Rose Inn in the 1960s and '70s were blamed on this harmless spectre. Why a mourning maid should behave herself for two hundred years and then become a raging pyromaniac is inexplicable.

1915 At Windsor Court Private James Allagan of the Coldstream Guards was charged with assaulting Joseph Fellows, Frederick Stone (licensee of the Globe public house at Windsor) and PC Tamlin while in the execution of his duty. Allagan was also charged with being drunk and disorderly. Arising out of the case was a summons against one Arthur Vickers for refusing to aid and assist a police constable. PC Tamlin, who had been considerably injured in the assault, stated that he had seen Allagan pick up a tin in Goswell Street and throw it at Mr Fellows. Witnesses stated that he then followed Allagan who later turned and threw a bottle at him; he then tried to effect an arrest. This failed when he was kicked in the groin and had his fingers forced up his nostrils. The prisoner escaped and was chased into Denmark Street, where Mr Stone tried to help subdue Allagan at PC Tamlin's request. The prisoner pushed his finger in Mr Stone's eye, causing great pain. Stone was also beaten severely by the prisoner's belt.

Mr Stone and PC Tamlin wrestled Allagan to the ground, but not before he had delivered a dozen or more kicks. Mr Fellows and Mr Stone then tried to keep Allagan pinned to the ground while PC Tamlin attempted to handcuff him. However, a man named Vickers, assisted by several others, pulled them

The opening of Reading Gaol was reputedly on 26 August 1793. Its predecesor, Old Castle Street Prison, had housed a treadmill, much like the one seen here. The old prison was unique in that the treadmill could be observed by passers-by.

Stately Windsor was shocked by the behaviour of William and Mary Smith who had been charged on 29 August 1830 with passing fraudulent coins in the town's public houses. (*Author's Collection*)

away, allowing Allagan to escape yet again. Traced to the barracks the next day Allagan was arrested. He was gaoled for four months for the assault on PC Tamlin and one month each on the Fellows and Stone charges; sentences to run consecutively. The drunk and disorderly charge was not proceeded with and the outcome of the Vickers summons is not recorded.

29 AUGUST **1830** At Windsor Police Courts William Smith and his common-law wife Mary were charged with attempting to pass two fraudulent coins at Windsor public houses. Both parties had tried to pass a half-crown and a shilling at the Royal Hotel and the Crown Inn in Peascod Street. The matter was judged to be so serious that it was passed to the quarter sessions. William Smith was sentenced to six months in gaol and Mary Smith to two months.

30 AUGUST **1934** This day brought one of several reports of the sobbing woman at the Bull Hotel at Wargrave. A former landlady of the inn, she was reputed to have taken a lover. Unfortunately for the lady her husband caught them in a most embarrassing situation. Understandably upset, he banished her from the inn and refused to let her see her young child. According to folklore she was reported to have died of a broken heart. More likely she passed away from cold, hunger or suicide, but her ghost returned to the inn, where over the years she has been heard weeping. There was at one time wallpaper in the Teardrop Room that was said to be stained by the woman's tears.

31 AUGUST **1633** It was reported on this day that Ludvic Bowyer had his ears nailed to the Reading pillory. He also had the letters L&R (Liar and Rogue) branded on his forehead.

SEPTEMBER

Cumnor Hall, where Amy Robsart met with a fatal accident on 8 September 1560. Her ghost haunted the house until it was demolished in 1810.

1 SEPTEMBER **1782** This was the day that George and Joseph Weston made a final attempt to escape from Newgate Prison, before being hanged there two days later. On a cold night in 1781 the Weston brothers robbed the Royal Mail at Maidenhead Thicket. The Royal Mail was not a streamlined coach with six cantering horses; it was a horse and trap with a drowsy post boy. At 3 a.m. George rode down and placed his gun at the post boy's head. Instead of complying with George's order to dismount the boy started screaming and shouting. Weston struck the boy on the side of the head. Then he struck him again and pulled him off the cart. Joseph joined him and the pair rode to a lonely field at Lot's Farm, near Twyford, to divvy up the loot. This was the only time in their ten-year career of highway robbery, fraud, burglary, housebreaking and skulduggery that the brothers had used violence. With a history that would put Frank and Jesse James to shame the two men had swindled and thieved their way through half the towns in England. They had also been chased to and from the continent. It was, however, the Maidenhead mail robbery that made them famous. The Lot's Farm share-out was £10,000. A rough guess at today's equivalent would be in the region of £3 million. However it did not last them long; within months they had gambled it away or spent it on members of the fairer sex. Their high spending was to be their downfall.

The Weston brothers' brief but colourful lives were ended at Tyburn. This image by Hogarth illustrates the popularity of such events.

Windsor Police arrested Charles Scott when he walked into the police station and said: 'I have killed my wife. I have stabbed her with a knife and cut her throat with a razor.' *(Berkshire County Library)*

A merciless and relentless Jack Clarke, the famed Bow Street runner, had been on the brothers' trail for some time, doggedly watching and waiting to pounce; and pounce Clarke and his colleagues did, on a smart hotel in Wardour Street. The brothers fled through the window but were caught in Soho Square, which in those days was a marshalling ground for sheep and cattle. After a short stay, and several escape attempts, the brothers walked to their deaths at Newgate on 3 September.

1891 At Newbury, Kesian Preston was accused of assaulting Alice Norway at Lambourn. Preston, Alice Norway's brother-in-law, sent a message for her to meet him. On meeting, Preston rushed at Alice and knocked her to the ground while her brother punched her incessantly. She was taken from the scene, badly bloodied by her husband. It was later discovered that 6*d* had been taken from her pocket. Preston was fined £5. The brother was not found.

2 September

1899 At 3 a.m. PC Garwood was manning the desk at Windsor police station, when suddenly the door was thrust open and a young man came in bleeding profusely from a cut eye. 'I have killed my wife,' he stated. 'I have stabbed her with a knife and cut her throat with a razor.' The young man, Charles Scott, was well known to the Windsor police. PC Garwood despatched two other constables (Taylor and Coombes) to 39 South Place, Scott's abode. At the address the two young constables found the body of Eliza O'Shea, Scott's common-law wife. A Dr Wyburn was called, who quickly ascertained the cause of death was by severance of the larynx. There were also multiple stab wounds. Charles Scott was charged with the murder of Eliza O'Shea at 7 p.m.; he appeared for trial at Reading on 5 November. The jury heard the long and passionate story of Scott and Eliza O'Shea. It was a story of

3 September

extremes, of love and hate, of jealousy, revenge and violence. It appeared that the couple could not exist with or without each other. In fact Scott did not have to live long without his Eliza. Found guilty of murder, he was hanged at Reading on 28 November.

4 SEPTEMBER **1836** The pretty little town of Wallingford must have been a dangerous place to live in 1836. It was announced on this day that the town had found it necessary to appoint three new constables of the watch. They would each be provided with a glazed hat, a greatcoat, a rattle, a blunderbuss and a brace of pistols.

5 SEPTEMBER **1853** At Maidenhead Borough Bench George Newberry, the boots at Cliveden Hotel, was charged with stealing cigars from that establishment. The manager of the hotel said that he had lost twenty cigars worth *2s 6d* and some butterscotch, and went on to describe circumstances that left no doubt that Newberry was the thief. Newberry was fined £1.

6 SEPTEMBER **1940** On this day it was decided to drain the Arborfield pond and lay it with grass. When the workmen drained the water a large white stone appeared. As the men went to move it, there arose a hue and cry from the villagers. The workmen were persuaded to backfill rather than disturb the stone. It transpired that in the eighteenth century a witch was pestering Arborfield; a farmer's wife on the Reading Road said she could turn into a cat at will. She also spirited away sheep and cows, turned placid dogs mad, caused milk to curdle and brought down torrents of rain that destroyed local crops. When the poor lady was accused of causing winds that blew off the local councillor's wig, something had to be done. The woman was taken,

Do not disturb the ground over the pond at Arborfield. The witch buried beneath the giant stone may return to wreak havoc on the village. (*Les Howard*)

bound and thrown in the pond to drown. Having put paid to the witch's life, one would have thought the story ended – but no! The old lady's ghost rose from the still waters on many occasions. The village elders held a meeting and decided to place a large stone on her body. Whether or not the haunting ended is not recorded, but one can understand the locals' reluctance to move the stone even in the enlightened 1940s. In 2000 a local firm cutting the grass here had a great many inexplicable things go wrong with their equipment, so who knows?

1890 On this evening the young curate of Cranbourne, near Windsor, went **8 September** for a stroll. The young man was new to the area and spent his evenings exploring the many paths of Windsor Forest. On this particular evening the curate came across a disused shed or barn. Peeping through a gap in the boards, the curate saw the strange sight of a dozen local teenage girls, semi-clad and spinning to a strange humming sound. The curate, finding the whole situation most perturbing, was quick to inform the parents. He was surprised at their reaction. He was either told to mind his own business or that he was working too hard and imagining things. On approaching the vicar, the curate was told to say nothing as it was only children playing games. Unheedful of the vicar's advice the curate made further enquiries and several nights later the young man was once again at the shed. What happened next is unknown but the curate was found late that night at Moss End, Warfield. He was dishevelled, semi-conscious and had been badly beaten. The curate would, or could, not say what had happened to him, but a short time later local girls contrived against him and accused him of immoral behaviour. Sacked from the Church, the young man took to the road. He played the flute at fairs and spent some time in prison. The authorities must have forgiven him because he later became a clergyman in Kent. However, he would never divulge what happened to him that night in a Berkshire village.

1560 Prior to its demolition in 1810 Cumnor Hall was home to the ghost of Amy Robsart. On 8 September 1560 Amy's body was found at the bottom of a flight of stairs. Apparently her neck had been broken by an accidental fall. Unfortunately for Amy she was in the way of Robert Dudley's (her husband) ambitions. Dudley was a favourite of Elizabeth I. It was a serendipitous occurrence for Dudley that Amy met her death in such a fashion. Gossip and suspicion was rife; but proof of murder was in short supply. Dudley was made Earl of Leicester and remained the Queen's favourite until his death in 1588. The story goes that shortly before his death he met the ghost of Amy in Wychwood Forest. The ghost warned that they would meet soon. They probably did, for Dudley took a chill and died soon afterwards.

1851 On this day in Faringdon the town crier announced that a reward **9 September** would be offered to anyone who could supply information as to the where-abouts of a stolen plum cake. Details emerged that Elizabeth Saunders, aged sixteen, had been seen eating a cake near her back door, but had run away when challenged; Constable Tables had found cake crumbs on her windowsill. Saunders was charged at Reading and reprimanded about her behaviour.

10 SEPTEMBER **1867** Mark Dowling, William Collins, John Brown, Francis Wilmot, Harry Wheatland and John Fry were each fined 1s for letting their ponies and donkeys stray on the highway between Crookham Common and Brimpton.

11 SEPTEMBER **1754** On or about this day at Newbury Sarah Deacon, who had an illegitimate child, was sent to a house of correction for a month and was ordered to be publicly whipped every Friday between 2 and 3 p.m.

12 SEPTEMBER **1538** Thomas Barrie, an inmate of Donnington Hospital, was sentenced at Newbury to stand in the Market Place with his ears nailed to the pillory. Afterwards they were to be cut off.

13 SEPTEMBER **1869** Alice Kaye, a female patient, slipped over the lower wall of Broadmoor Asylum and disappeared without trace. The apparent ease of the lady's escape meant that the wall was raised to 16½ft. Alice was the institution's last inmate to abscond over the wall.

14 SEPTEMBER **1915** This morning brought a sad case to Slough Court. Jessie Mibus, aged forty-five, was accused of attempted murder and attempted suicide. The unfortunate woman had taken her eight-year-old son Harold into her arms and turned on the gas. She had also cut her left wrist. The pair were saved by PC Becket, who had called to deliver a summons to Harold for stealing objects from neighbours. Apparently Jessie could not stand the shame. Mother and son were placed in the workhouse for six weeks until the charge was raised at Reading. Alas, there is no further information recorded about this case.

15 SEPTEMBER **1890** Henry Page was charged with wilful damage to a police cell at Newbury. Chief Inspector Bennet stated that Page was in custody charged with stealing a coat. The charge was later dropped, but while he was in that Newbury police cell he was the worst prisoner they had ever had. He swore, broke his bed, scraped the walls and spat at officers. Newbury police had since heard from Bristol, Page's home town, to the effect that Page was an incorrigible rogue and had four previous convictions in the area.

16 SEPTEMBER **1831** At Windsor, Samual Solloway sued John Cooper for assault and employing a boy to follow him and call him names. Cooper was fined 2s.

17 SEPTEMBER **1831** At Maidenhead County Bench Court John Blacrall was accused of ill-treating a donkey at Bray (no pun intended). A lady of substance deposed that she had witnessed a man (Blacrall) striking a donkey across the nostrils

with a stick. She had fetched a young gentleman, Knowle Holme, who relieved Blacrall of the stick and verbally remonstrated with him. Blacrall's language then became so offensive that they fetched a constable. Blacrall was found guilty and fined 5s plus 8s 4d costs.

1900 This day brought another report of a haunting by a guardsman at Long Walk, near Windsor Castle. The ghost had appeared to three separate walkers on three consecutive days. Some years previously a young Grenadier Guards recruit who saw a ghost on Long Walk had been so frightened that he shot himself. Some weeks later a guardsman, about to relieve his comrade on sentry duty, was visited by the ghost of the guardsman who had shot himself. Terrified, he proceeded to take over from his colleague who was in much the same condition, having seen the ghostly guardsman minutes before.

18 SEPTEMBER

'MAD PARSON' RELEASED

Famous Escape from Broadmoor Recalled

THE Home Secretary, Mr. Chuter Ede, has signed an order for the release from the Broadmoor Institution of John Edward Allen, who, after his escape from the Institution in July, 1947, became known as the "Mad Parson."

Allen, who is 39 years old, was certified insane and sent to Broadmoor in 1937 after he had been sentenced to death for child murder at Oxford. He took part in amateur theatricals there and escaped in 1947 dressed as a parson.

He remained at liberty for 22 months, during which period he secured a number of well-paid jobs. When he was recaptured he was earning £11 a week as a baker.

In Care of Friends

He wrote to the medical superintendent at Broadmoor and to newspapers during his liberty protesting that he was no longer insane. His conduct when he was free from restraint was taken into consideration by Home Office experts when they were consid-

1951 News came in that the Home Secretary, Mr Chuter Ede, had signed the release from Broadmoor of John Edward Allen, 'The Mad Parson'. Allen had earned the nickname from the national papers during his escape in 1947. At a concert party produced by the Broadhumorists, Allen took the part of a vicar during a sketch. Near the end of the entertainments, Allen, still dressed in his ecclesiastical attire, slipped into the darkness and disappeared. Next day the canteen was checked and it was discovered that a goodly supply of food had disappeared along with 'The Parson'. Allen was free for many months. When finally caught he was working as a waiter in a West Country restaurant. On his return to Broadmoor it was discovered that he had proved to have been extremely sane and sound of mind during nearly two years of freedom. He had also held down some well-paid and responsible jobs. 'The Mad Parson' was not released without some controversy. It was pointed out that he had entered Broadmoor in 1937 after murdering a child in Oxford.

19 SEPTEMBER

The release of the 'Mad Parson' from Broadmoor.
(*Wokingham Times*)

20 SEPTEMBER **1787** This is one of the days that brought gold hunters to the west of Berkshire. It had long been a legend at Little Wittenham that the nearby Sinodun Hill contained buried treasure. On the top of the hill an old Roman fort had once stood, and according to folklore the 'Money Pit' was full of Roman valuables. A story relates that one villager had dug deeply in the pit and found an iron chest. As he was about to open it, a raven alighted on it and cried: 'He is not born yet.' Being a devout man and taking this to be a sign that he was not the chosen one, the villager replaced the chest and refilled the hole. In September 1787 a local landowner heard the story and hired two men to dig; they found nothing, but word spread encouraging many fortune-seekers.

21 SEPTEMBER **1816** At Caversham an autopsy was performed on a dog, which had 'gone mad' and bitten three people at nearby Mapledurham. The results showed that the dog (brought into town by a group of tramps) was not affected by hydrophobia (rabies). It did, however, have long worms in its stomach. A village fund was set up to raise sufficient money to send the victims to Southampton, where they could bathe their injuries in salt water.

22 SEPTEMBER **1944** The body of a man was found on the railway track at Crowthorne. The dead man was a depressive, who had lost his lodgings at Bracknell and had been refused admittance at Wokingham Hospital. At the Coroner's Court a verdict of misadventure was recorded. What would seem something of a mystery is the suggestion by the coroner that the victim had been accidentally struck by a train while his mind had been on other matters.

23 SEPTEMBER **1834** At Reading, Charles Merriet was convicted of stealing a bushel of wheat from a Wantage farmer. The wheat was discovered wrapped in a red cloth behind a withy tree. William Taylor, foreman at the farm, informed the court that he had discovered the wheat after he found some missing from a sack. He and a constable had lain in wait that evening and arrested Merriet when he came to retrieve it. Finding Merriet guilty the judge sentenced him to one month's hard labour. A case against Margaret Britton, a local publican, who had previously bought wheat from Merriet for 9*d*, was dropped.

24 SEPTEMBER **1834** On this day Thomas Rogers and his son John were travelling from Easton to Reading. They had been working in the fields and, as it was an extremely hot day, they had removed their shirts. On their journey Thomas Rogers offered a lift to the Barkis brothers, William and George, itinerant workers who had been helping out at the same farm as the Rogerses. Rogers dropped the pair at a tent, which was their makeshift abode. On returning home Thomas Rogers discovered that both his and his son's shirts were missing. A constable was called and the Barkises's abode was searched. The shirts were discovered behind a flowerpot. At court in October William Barkis was sentenced to two month's hard labour and his brother George to four months.

1815 This was one of the days concerned in a spate of sightings of ghostly hounds at Darrell's Style, near Great Shefford. A summary of the often-told tale is as follows:

On a rainy day in November 1575 Mrs Barnes, the midwife of Great Shefford, was taken from her home by coach. She had been blindfolded and remained so until entering the bedroom of a vast house, where a lady in a mask was in the last throes of giving birth. The midwife assisted but as the baby boy was born a ferocious-looking man grabbed the child and threw it on to an open fire until the tiny life was extinguished. During the confusion Mrs Barnes took the chance of cutting some of the bed draping before she returned home. It did not take long for the old lady to work out that the only large house she could have been driven to in that time was Littlecote and that the fierce-looking man was Wild Will Darrell. Who the masked lady was is open to conjecture, for many and various have been the names put forward, including Wild Will's sister. Either from fear or because of the relatively wealthy lifestyle she had suddenly developed, Mrs Barnes said nothing! Nothing, that is, until she was on her deathbed. There, in the presence of several men of the cloth, she told all. Subsequently Darrell was arrested, charged and found not guilty, English justice at the time being the best that money could buy. He did not, however, escape divine vengeance. Darrell met his death while out riding.

Wild Will Darrell threw a newborn baby on the fire at Littlecote. (*Berkshire County Library*)

He was thrown from his horse near a style (later known as Darrell's Style). Some say his horse shied at the sight of a burning baby.

26 SEPTEMBER   **1348**   This was the time that the Black Death was at its most widespread. Berkshire lost over a third of its population, including Thomas de Brackeles, vicar of Sonning; Sonning, being a ferry point, was extremely badly hit. The name Black Death was said to come from the darkening of the skin – caused by an internal haemorrhage (ecchymosis or bruise). Coughing and sneezing were other symptoms, hence:

> Ring a ring o'roses
> A pocket full of posies
> A-Tishoo! A-Tishoo!
> We all fall down.

27 SEPTEMBER   **1601**   On this day the proud people of Hungerford announced that, at their own expense, they had built a town hall, a shop, a corn market and two prisons. Why two prisons for a population of only about 1,200 remains a mystery.

28 SEPTEMBER   **1891**   At the Borough Police Court in Newbury Thomas Stanley, a cripple, was charged with begging. George Withers deposed that Stanley had come into his shop asking for money. Withers ordered Stanley to leave but he was drunk and wouldn't go. After some argument Stanley went but returned within an hour and a half. Sergeant Seagrove stated that he had been called to the shop

Sonning, one of the county's prettiest villages. In 1348 it lost 40 per cent of its inhabitants to the Black Death. (*Brenda Allaway*)

and found the prisoner drunk, threatening and abusive. Stanley eventually collapsed and was carried on a stretcher to the police station. En route he woke up kicking and screaming. Sergeant Seagrove had to request the assistance of two labourers to restrain him. Stanley was found guilty and sentenced to one month's imprisonment.

1883 At Upton Lea, near Slough, five-year-old Florence Lisa Adams died a horrendous death, after being dragged along by a horse-drawn roller. Much was made at the Coroner's Court of the driver riding the horse instead of leading it. The sorrowing parents put forward the point of view that had the horse been led the workman would have heard Florence's screams. The man replied that he had heard many screams that day from a crowd of children who had followed his vehicle. He also refuted Mr Adams's insinuation that he was drunk; he had not had more than a pint all day. Mr Adams withdrew his accusation. The coroner gave his condolences before announcing that the jury had passed a verdict of accidental death.

29 September

1865 George Ewins, respected landlord of the Crooked Billet near Wokingham, was charged with attempting to commit suicide. It had not been a good year for George. In January he had been in court, on the side of the prosecution. Ewins had charged William Goddard, Thomas Edwards and James Brown (three broom-dashers) with assault. Brown was also charged

30 September

The Crooked Billet near Wokingham, where depressed landlord George Ewins attempted suicide by jumping down his own well. Unfortunately for George, the well was dry and he only succeeded in breaking his ankle. (*Brenda Allaway*)

with assaulting the landlord's wife. The charges were dropped because the complainant, George Ewins, was intoxicated in court and mostly incoherent. A little later in the year Ewins, together with George Miles, landlord of the Spotted Cow, and one George Bowens were charged with riotous behaviour and fined 5s each. Miles was also charged with opening a beerhouse before noon on a Sunday and was fined 20s. On 30 September Ewins explained to Wokingham Court that he had attempted suicide by jumping down his well. Unfortunately there was no water owing to a drought. He sustained a broken ankle and remained in that uncomfortable condition overnight. The judge took a dim view of the tittering in court as he bound Ewins over.

OCTOBER

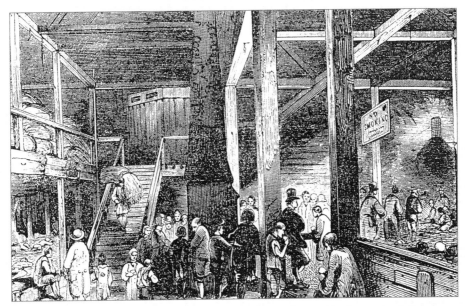

An artist's impression of a workhouse, similar to that at Easthampstead. James
Henderson, an inhabitant of Easthampstead workhouse, met an untimely end
on 7 October 1883.

1 OCTOBER **1797** On this day one local paper reported the murder of Edward Bunce, a turnpike-keeper of Coppid Beech Hill, Wokingham. The report was very brief and stated that the unfortunate man had been shot in the head while on duty in the early hours of the morning. The authorities were offering a reward for information concerning two men, one in a blue coat, the other in a brown one. Both were of stocky build and swarthy of feature. This was the entire and sole report on the subject. Whether or not the suspects were ever apprehended will remain a mystery.

1629 This is also believed to be the day that two outhouses of the Garter Inn at Windsor were set on fire by an eight-year-old boy. John Dean was found guilty and hanged for his crime. He is reputed to be the youngest person ever to be executed in England.

2 OCTOBER **1851–1951** The *Bracknell Yearbook*, brought out in 1951 to commemorate the centenary of the village church, mentions the exploits of one landlord in the 1770s and his novel way of disposing of guests. Unnamed in the report the landlord and his wife kept the Hind's Head in Bracknell. The hostelry had been there long before the town developed. In all probability it was a couple of houses at a turnpike on the Ascot to Reading Road. Be that as it may, the place soon developed a terrible reputation. Road users went for miles to avoid it and coaches would pay their fare at the turnpike and swiftly move on. It was rumoured that people who stayed the night stayed forever, their bodies being launched down a deep well. The landlord had a bed with a spring-loaded trapdoor leading to a cellar. After plying his guests with drink he would spring the trapdoor and cudgel them to death in the cellar below. He is said to have been helped in this enterprise by his wife and several regulars. It is said that he was only caught because a barmaid took a fancy to a young traveller and warned him. The traveller got together a group of farmers who raided the place and arrested five of those present. All were hanged at Reading. This is a terribly frustrating tale based mostly on folklore. There is no record of these hangings at Reading. Another version has it set in the 1850s but this time with no executions because the landlord committed suicide and his wife went to a mental institution. However, when the old place was demolished in about 1963 bones were found in the well; it is a pity they were canine and feline!

The *Bracknell Yearbook*, published in 1951, tells of horrendous murders at the Hind's Head. (*Bracknell News*)

3 OCTOBER **1850** It was announced that 30 in every 1,000 people in Reading had died from typhus and other diseases. This was double the rate of the rest of England.

INSPECTOR EAST KILLED IN MAIDENHEAD

Tragic Death of Well-Known Wokingham Personality

The untimely death, under very tragic circumstances, of Inspector Francis John East, at Maidenhead on Wednesday October 4th has come as a shock to his many friends throughout the Berkshire constabulary area, and particularly in Wokingham, where he was a popular figure.

While the circumstances under which he met his death are still obscure, the facts at present available show that before he was discovered lying in the road at the bottom of Castle Hill, Maidenhead, suffering from multiple injuries, at 11.30 p.m. on the Wednesday night, from which he died without gaining consciousness, he had occasion to intervene

Inspector East as a young man

in a disturbance between two civilians and two American soldiers in the High Street

(Reading Chronicle)

1868 Also on this day the *Berkshire Chronicle* informed the population that a Broadmoor lunatic, named Turner, was still at large. He was described as a powerful man weighing 15 stone, 6ft 2in tall and extremely violent. Rather stating the obvious the *Chronicle* went on to comment: 'The local residents will certainly feel better satisfied when they hear of his recapture.'

1944 Police Inspector John East was called to a fracas in Maidenhead. At Castle Hill the disturbance now seemed to be verbal. Some local youths were involved in a slanging match with two American soldiers who were leaning on a weapons transporter. The sight of Inspector East calmed the situation; he took the names of the Americans and then turned to do the same with the locals. Seeing this as an opportunity to escape, the two GIs (Styles and Phillips) shot away up Castle Hill in their vehicle. Deciding to ask more questions East jumped on to the running board. He fell off some 400yds further on and his body was crushed by a speeding car. Inspector Francis John East, aged forty-one, died of his injuries minutes later. At the court martial damning evidence came to the fore. Of all the injuries on East's body a bruise on his jaw was not consistent with his other injuries. It was decided that Styles and Phillips had knocked

4 OCTOBER

Castle Hill, Maidenhead. *(Brenda Allaway)*

him off the vehicle, contrary to their evidence claiming they had tried to hang on to him to prevent him falling. Both men were found guilty; each received a dishonourable discharge and three years' hard labour.

5 OCTOBER 1944 On this day three or four military policemen were socialising with the locals at the Crown Hotel at Kingsclere. At about 8 p.m. some ten US servicemen entered the establishment. They were approached by two of the MPs, Anderson and Coates, who asked them for their passes. Being unable to produce their documents the servicemen were sent back to their quarters. It was nearing closing time at 10 p.m. when shots could be heard from outside. Private Anderson went to the door to remonstrate, whereupon he was immediately cut down by a volley of bullets. Private Coates, already wounded by several bullets, jumped through a window and ran towards the firing. He was shot down by a hail of bullets and died in the square. As bullets ricocheted all around the inn the locals 'hit the floor'. Mrs Rose Napper clutched her face and screamed. A few seconds later she lay dead. Private Washington, another MP, returned fire from a place of concealment, badly wounding two of the attacking servicemen. Finally they retreated. The inquest at Thatcham town hall was heard in November, although very little of the evidence seeped out. A sure and certain blackout descended on the whole inquiry. The result, however, is known. A statement was issued informing the public that nine American servicemen had been sentenced to life imprisonment.

Hushed up during the Second World War: three people were slaughtered at the Crown, Kingsclere, by American GIs. (*Peter Bourne*)

6 OCTOBER 1799 This day brought some very sad news from the tiny village of Shottesbrooke. A popular village man was killed at Knowl Hill when a vast wall of peat he had been digging fell upon him.

7 OCTOBER 1883 A strange story unfolded in the village of Crowthorne. A labourer, Robert Cole, was travelling through the forest from Roundshill to Crowthorne. As he passed through Hagthorn, a very dark and depressing part of the woods, he noticed a badly decomposed body under a fallen tree. Cole sprinted to Crowthorne where he gabbled his story to an acquaintance. A police officer was approached and the three returned to Hagthorn with a barrow. Under the officer's instructions the rotting body was transported to the Crowthorne Inn, where it remained all night awaiting the coroner. The corpse was identified the following morning by the number on the remaining shreds of clothing. Mr J.P. McNillance, an officer at Easthampstead workhouse,

The Crowthorne Inn where the badly decayed remains of James Henderson were delivered by wheelbarrow to lie in state in the bar parlour. (*Brenda Allaway*)

identified the remnants as those issued to James Henderson in May. McNillance stated that Henderson had been delivered to the workhouse after being stuck up a tree for three days. He was a self-styled preacher and used high trees as makeshift pulpits. His home was at Katesgrove Road in Reading, where he lived as a widower with two young daughters. Henderson was forty-nine years of age. But how did he die? Coroner Weedon brought an open verdict: suicide, murder or accident; it certainly wasn't from natural causes.

1891 At Newbury Amelia Tuck was summoned for using obscene language in Bartholomew Street. Sergeant Borlass stated that as he and a constable escorted a male prisoner to the station Tuck's language was appalling. Tuck, who was a relative of the prisoner, was warned about her language but it only worsened. She was fined £1 or sentenced to fourteen days in prison.

8 OCTOBER

1891 On this day near Buckland, in the county of Berkshire, PC Portchmouth arrested Lucy Jordan on the Bampton Road. He took her into custody for the concealment of a birth and for suffocating the child by pushing her fingers down its throat. Apparently Lucy had given birth while her two sisters, who slept in the same bed, got up to make tea. Jordan received two years' hard labour at Reading Gaol.

9 OCTOBER

1892 At Newbury on this day the following were presented before the coroner Thomas Coke: John Cheyney, Godfrey Sweinton, John Pryhett, George Tyler, Richard Frankelyn and William Bedford, all of East Woodhay. They were accused, together with John Clayton and Thomas Edwards, of assaulting Robert Parys. Cheyney was also accused of attacking Parys with a sword, worth 5s, and giving him two wounds to the head. Parys died four days later. All were discharged but Cheyney got an official warning.

10 OCTOBER

1932 Ernest Hutchinson gave a second statement to the police about the murder of Mrs Gwen Warren at Heywood Park, Maidenhead, on 12 September 1932.

11 OCTOBER

The *Reading Standard*'s report on the murder of Gwen Warren.

Hutchinson had been Gwen's lodger when he was out of work and her bedfellow when he was gainfully employed. Things had looked bad for Ernest Hutchinson. Shortly after Gwen's disappearance he had sold her furniture and taken to the road, finally being arrested at Southend. Ernest Hutchinson's trial at Reading on 14 October attracted a vast crowd, many of whom came to see Sir Bernard Spilsbury, the world-famous pathologist. Spilsbury referred to the post mortem, saying the body had sustained many blows with a blunt object, but death had been caused by asphyxiation brought about by mattresses being piled on top of the victim. Hutchinson was found guilty and hanged at Oxford Prison.

E READING STANDARD. SATURDAY

MURDER TRIAL IN READING

Sentence of Death Passed on Maidenhead Baker.

HOW ACCUSED RECEIVED THE VERDICT.

As he entered the dock at the Berkshire Assizes on Friday arraigned for the murder of Gwendoline Annie Warren, 36, a married woman, of Haywood Avenue, White Waltham, Maidenhead, who had been living apart from her husband, Ernest Hutchinson, 42, a baker, looked round the court and smiled. Throughout the trial his attitude was one of apparent unconcern, and during the hearing of the evidence he frequently smiled. He was quite unmoved when the grim and sordid details of the discovery of the unhappy woman's body hidden in a bedroom was related. On Saturday afternoon Hutchinson smiled when the jury returned the verdict of guilty, and he laughed softly as Mr. Justice MacKinnon passed sentence of death. The Judge's voice shook with emotion, but Hutchinson, as he heard his doom pronounced, smiled broadly, and was still smiling as he left the dock.

The trial aroused a good deal of interest, and large crowds have assembled each day outside the Assize Courts. Many who were unable to obtain admission waited outside to hear the result of the trial and to watch the departure of the Judge. Inside the crowded Court was a fair sprinkling of women.

THE FINAL SCENES.

12 OCTOBER

1915 At Windsor Children's Court before the mayor, Councillor Carter, two eight-year-old boys were charged with throwing stones and giving a police constable false names. One stone had gone through a window and could have caused injury. The mayor gave them an official warning and stated that if they were brought before the court again they would be whipped, and would they be good enough to pass this message on to their school friends.

13 OCTOBER

1891 William Sage, alias William Stevens, a 48-year-old painter, was charged at Newbury with two offences of obtaining money under false pretences. Mr William Bollard stated that Sage had requested £3 from him while he looked for work. He went on to tell the court that Sage had informed him that he had inherited £3,000 and that a solicitor would soon arrive with £150. Joseph and Hester Harris of Jack Street, where Sage lodged, told a similar story. He was found guilty. Information was subsequently received from Glastonbury and Bristol of numerous similar charges. Sage was sentenced to three years' penal servitude.

14 OCTOBER

1834 At the Michaelmas Sessions in front of Lord Downshire, John Miles of Donnington was convicted of stealing 5s in ha'pennies. As this was the prisoner's third offence he was transported for seven years.

15 OCTOBER

1810 The *Reading Mercury* reported an inquest that was held at the Horse and Groom, at Bracknell, concerning the body of William Ware. The unfortunate

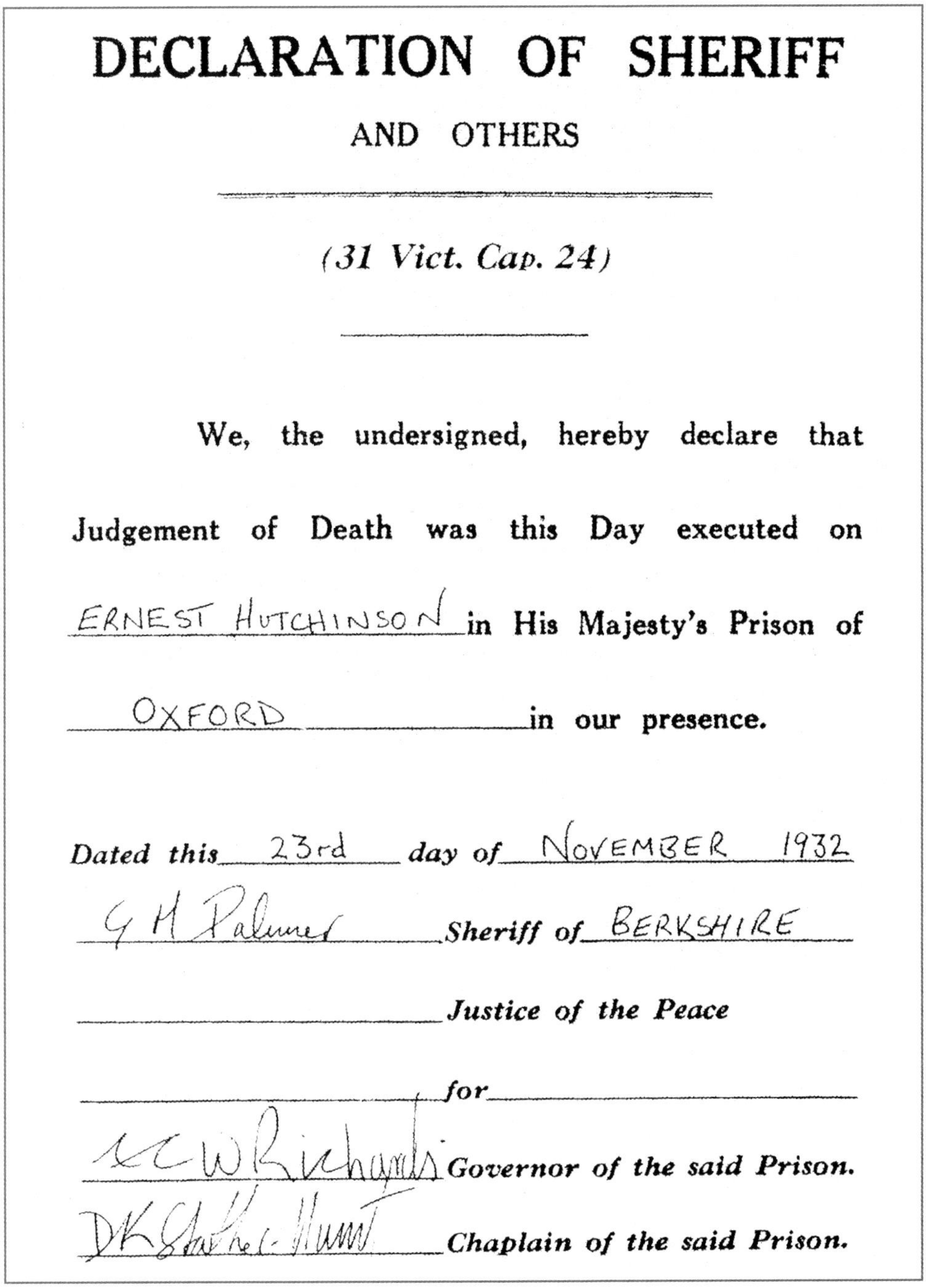

DECLARATION OF SHERIFF

AND OTHERS

(31 Vict. Cap. 24)

We, the undersigned, hereby declare that

Judgement of Death was this Day executed on

ERNEST HUTCHINSON in His Majesty's Prison of

OXFORD in our presence.

Dated this __23rd__ day of __NOVEMBER 1932__

G H Palmer Sheriff of __BERKSHIRE__

_____ **Justice of the Peace**

_____ **for** _____

C W Richards **Governor of the said Prison.**

D K Stretch-Hunt **Chaplain of the said Prison.**

The sheriff's declaration of Ernest Hutchinson's execution. (*Maidenhead Advertiser*)

youth (aged seventeen) was returning to Frimley from Bracknell fair with his father and two friends when the party were set upon by three men, thought to be Irish, who beat them with cudgels for some considerable time. The unhappy party returned to the inn where William later died of his wounds. The jury brought in a verdict of wilful murder by persons unknown.

1834 At a Maidenhead court Richard William Wheeler was charged with stealing two trusses of hay from his employer, Solomon Codd of Bray.

16 OCTOBER

Magistrates praised a local constable for his powers of observation. He had followed a trail of hay to the defendant's cottage. Wheeler was found guilty and sentenced to fourteen days' hard labour.

17 OCTOBER   **1835** Huntley Robinson was tried at Reading Michaelmas sessions for stealing 1s. He had fraudulently tried to obtain the money from a wealthy Mr Poco by forging a note from his employer. It was pointed out by local constables that although Robinson had only just turned sixteen he was an incorrigible rogue with a long history of petty crime. He was found guilty and sentenced to one year's imprisonment.

18 OCTOBER   **1918** At 1.40 p.m. on this date Mrs Ada Edge was walking along Love Lane towards Shaw when she was startled and terrified by a young man who ran out of a field. He was covered in blood and bleeding profusely from a gash on his throat. The wound seemed to make him incapable of speech. He gesticulated towards the field. At that moment Frederick Schelling, a Swiss baker who was making his deliveries, came across the scene. All three of them entered the meadow, where they saw a horrendous sight. A young woman and a tiny child lay dead with their throats cut. At 2.15 p.m. Dr Hemsted arrived on the scene and performed an emergency tracheotomy that saved the young man's life. At the ensuing inquest at Donnington parish hall it emerged that the woman was Sarah Rose, a gypsy living under canvas at Enborne, the tiny child was her six-month-old daughter Isabella and the man, now in intensive care at Newbury Hospital, was Sarah's cousin and husband Joseph Rose. In a letter from Newbury Hospital Rose stated that he had been eating in a field with Sarah and Isabella when a man appeared with a knife. Sarah obviously knew the man because she screamed: 'No! No! Harry – please don't.' It was to no avail, as the man attacked all three leaving Sarah and Isabella dead and Rose dying. Dr Hemsted took the stand for over an hour. He described in detail the wounds of each and also said that he found it strange that Joseph Rose had three tiny cuts on his throat apart from the one that so nearly brought about his demise. It was decided to charge Rose with two counts of murder and one of attempted suicide. Unfortunately the case was again suspended as Rose, who had recovered from the cut throat, was now at death's door with influenza. Proceedings finally recommenced on 16 January 1919. Circumstantial evidence was very strong against Rose. Firstly a sharp pocket knife was found in his pocket and secondly he had no wounds on his arms or wrists. Surely, the prosecution suggested, a man would try to protect his wife and daughter. But by far the most damning evidence came from Dr Hemsted, who stated that the three minor wounds on Rose's throat, in all probability, came from three practice cuts before trying a deeper one. Joseph Rose, aged twenty-five, was found guilty and hanged at Oxford on 17 February 1919.

19 OCTOBER   **1891** At the Berkshire quarter sessions Alfred Bowshier was charged with indecently assaulting Louisa Thatcher, aged fourteen, at Woodhay. Bowshier was found guilty and sentenced to ten months' hard labour.

1891 Once again at the Berkshire quarter sessions Jane Brinsmead, aged thirty-seven, was found guilty of stealing a jacket and petticoat at Wokingham. Brinsmead, who had a long history of crime, was sentenced to eighteen month's penal servitude.

20 OCTOBER

1856 On this day the Sandhurst Village Council made an order to the Treasurer of the Overseers of Thornton, Buckinghamshire, for £3 – the cost arising from the upkeep of Alice Carr, a lunatic, from 12 May to 29 September and her subsequent transportation to Littlemore Asylum. The Overseers at Thornton queried the bill; they thought the cost of feeding one woman for 4½ months a little excessive.

21 OCTOBER

1916 Army drivers Charles Sharman and William Hulatt were charged at Maidenhead with stealing copper worth 10*s* from Richard Lewis and selling it for 2*s* to John Fitter, a rag and bone man at Holyport. In court Fitter protested that he had bought the copper in good faith at the Cross Keys at Maidenhead. Sharman was found not guilty, Hulatt was found guilty and bound over with £5 in default and Fitter received fourteen days' hard labour.

22 OCTOBER

1830 On this day at the magistrates meeting at Windsor town hall a carrier named Piers was charged with fraudulently robbing Lady Harcourt of 2*s*. The carrier had delivered a parcel after altering the charge to nearly double. The carrier was found guilty and received a sentence of seven days' hard labour.

23 OCTOBER

1830 At the Coroner's Court in Windsor town hall, Mr Henry George said that on the previous Saturday he had been walking at the Long Walk, Windsor, when he heard a noise like a body falling from a tree. He ran to the spot where the noise came from and found the deceased, Joseph Summers, lying with his face to the ground and not breathing. Leaving the body in the company of a young man who was walking in the vicinity, George set off to contact a surgeon, Mr Holderness, who lived nearby. On their return he found Mrs Summers, the deceased's wife, weeping near the body. Mr Holderness stated that he had returned with George to view the body and found that the deceased had fractured his collarbone, his nose, his face and his spine. All of the injuries were consistent with falling from a tree. Mrs Summers stated that she had left her husband, who was seventy-five, climbing trees to gather firewood. The jury brought forth a verdict of accidental death.

24 OCTOBER

1800 On this day Mary Piggott of Lambourn was convicted with Joshua Smith of Chilton and charged with selling short measures of bread. Both bakers were fined 15*s* for selling half-gallon loaves 9oz short.

25 OCTOBER

1850 John Nash was charged at Maidenhead with using abusive language. Nash admitted that he had seen a man named Laves commit a felony by stealing a pair of boots. Nash had followed Laves to a Mrs Phipps' house where

26 OCTOBER

At tranquil Sandhurst in 1856 the Village Council charged Thornton Heath Council £3 for the upkeep of one of their lunatics, Alice Carr, from 12 May to 29 September. (*Kitty Dancy*)

he was staying, shouting 'Thief'. Robert Burn, a neighbour of Mrs Phipps, stated that he had heard Nash shouting to Laves: 'You are a rogue and a thief.' In his statement Nash had implied that his wife had come from Cookham that morning and had dropped a pair of boots she was carrying; he had seen Laves pick them up. Nash was fined 10s and bound over to keep the peace.

27 OCTOBER

1937 This was one of the days when the incredible phantom handprint appeared at the Royal Stag at Datchet. The story goes that at the end of the

nineteenth century a labourer drinking at the inn lost track of time and forgot his small son waiting outside. The weather was particularly bad and the poor lad froze to death in a snowdrift after continuously knocking at the window to attract his father's attention. The handprint seems to have appeared reasonably regularly and several quite good photographs have been taken.

The Royal Stag at Datchet, where the ghostly handprint of a freezing child regularly appears on the window. (*Peter Bourne*)

28 OCTOBER

1829 This day brought the death of the best apple grafter in England. After having warned others that his ladder was unsafe, William Napp proceeded to use it himself at Harwell. The ladder gave way, dropping Napp on to a paling. He died almost immediately. At the coroner's inquest, Mr Haffenden, a surgeon from Harwell, stated that Napp had broken all eight ribs on his right side and that the lung had been so lacerated that it allowed air to escape through the cellular membrane. Mr Napp was between seventy and eighty years old.

1830 On this day at Reading Mr Green, the Governor of Brixton Prison, **29 OCTOBER** stated that the prisons were becoming overrun with loose women and young boys. They served brief but frequent sentences, usually lasting between seven and twenty-one days. However, many re-offended. Mr Green knew of one prostitute who had been back to see him thirty times (albeit not on a professional basis). He went on to say that at Brixton the public flogging of women and young boys had cut down drastically the committing of further crimes. Mr Green also recommended solitary confinement. Mr Jackson thanked Mr Green for his talk and stated that his tactics would be employed vigorously at Reading Gaol.

1830 At a Windsor court William Smith was found guilty of passing a **30 OCTOBER** counterfeit coin at the Crown public house in Peascod Street. He was sentenced to six months' hard labour.

1829 On this day information was given by an 'informer' at Windsor that **31 OCTOBER** David Watts of Easthampstead was selling brooms without a licence. Watts was fined 10s. The informer was among a group of informers that was being escorted through Eton by the town's magistrates and constables. As per usual a mob of hissing and abusive locals followed the procession. One informer became a little separated from the rest. As part of the crowd was now in front of him he turned and fled back over the bridge to Windsor, followed by howls, bricks and screaming locals who were bent on doing him harm. Gaining the Berkshire side of the river the informer threw himself upon the protection of a nearby magistrate. The magistrate stated, possibly rather cowardly but quite correctly, that he was a Buckinghamshire magistrate and held no power as they were now in Berkshire.

The poor man turned to flee again, but too late: he was at the mercy of a mob. 'Throw him over,' and 'Duck him,' along with various other similar expressions of the intended *modus operandi* of his pursuers struck the frightened ears of the informer. This was by no means the only violence committed on the sensitive organs, as at proper intervals his ears were enlivened by hearty slaps by numerous old women. The wretch was then hurried to the waterside to suffer the crowd's happy intent of carrying out the ablutions.

A hilarious account was given in the *Windsor Express* of the poor wretch hanging on to gateposts and being stripped of his clothes with such wonderful phrases as 'clutched the rail with such strong grasp as to occasion some delay of loosening his hands; but so that time might not be absolutely lost while so doing he received in that position a few pails of water as preparatory of the ensuing ceremony'.

An informer was ambushed by local residents on Windsor Bridge. *(Berkshire County Library)*

On his way the hapless young man was thrown into the Brocas Ditch, 'A fine fetid receptacle for every variety of filth and rivalling in these respects the celebrated Clewer Ditch'. There the poor man was 'regaled for a while with the perfumes which exhaled from the rich compound of impurities'. Dragged out again the informer was then cast into the River Thames. The mob returned home satisfied that it had diligently performed its task.

NOVEMBER

The Rt Hon Lord Campbell, Lord Chief Justice, had no hesitation in sentencing Moses Hatto to death for the horrendous murder of Mary Anne Sturgeon, which had taken place on 1 November 1854.

1854 At 10.45 p.m. Mr Bunce was awakened by the noise of Moses Hatto throwing stones up at the window of Miss Sturgeon, the owner's maid. Hatto, a groom-manservant, was shouting, 'Mary Anne, Mary Anne, are you all right?'

On being joined by an irritated Bunce, Hatto explained that he had heard noises and believed they had been burgled and also that a horse had been stolen. It took the men only minutes to discover that a colt had gone missing and to find it grazing outside in the yard. Bunce reminded Hatto of the early hour they must rise and went back to bed.

Fifteen minutes later Farmer Goodwin, owner of Burnham Abbey farm, rode into the yard. He was surprised that there was no light in Mary Anne's room, as she usually got up to fix his supper at this time. Goodwin handed the reins to Hatto who looked dishevelled and whose trousers were exceedingly wet. Hatto explained upon inquiry that he had fallen in a puddle while looking for the colt with Bunce.

The farmer fixed himself a meal of bread, cheese and ale, vowing to have a word with Miss Sturgeon in the morning. Suddenly Goodwin heard footsteps overhead and smelled smoke. On investigation he found Hatto running with a bucket and smoke drifting from under Mary Anne's door. Yelling at Hatto to get help, Goodwin entered the room with a spare key. He was met by billows of black smoke. By this time his four other labourers were awake and passing up pail after pail of water. With the flames finally doused Goodwin discovered a body upon the bed, which was just recognisable as Mary Anne. Even in the half-light, however, Goodwin realised that her skull had been smashed. Sending his workers for help the farmer noticed something white on the burnt and bloodstained carpet. It was a tooth. At 2 a.m. Bunce arrived with Mr Haines, the doctor's assistant, and Mr Baldwin, a retired police officer, Burnham's only constable being out of town.

By 10 a.m. on 2 November PC John Eckford, the coroner Robert Eckford, Dr Roberts and Chief Constable Daniel Sexton of Maidenhead, together with a group of detectives, had all arrived at the farm. Taking an opportunity when Hatto was not around, Goodwin related several aspects of Hatto's strange behaviour.

At the Coroner's Court much of the evidence pointed to Hatto being the perpetrator of this horrendous crime. However, he stuck to his guns and swore it was the result of a burglary. One of the most damning bits of evidence came from another farmworker named Eggleton, who stated that he had delivered the first pail of water to Hatto outside the maid's door. He had been surprised that instead of throwing it into the room Hatto had dashed it to the floor and then bent down and washed his trousers with it.

At Hatto's trial on 9 November, nearly thirty witnesses were heard. In the intervening period Hatto had spent his time in Beaconsfield lock-up shouting abuse at all and sundry. He was found guilty and sentenced to death by Lord Campbell. While awaiting the hangman in Aylesbury Prison, Hatto had written a confession. Apparently the trouble had started when Mary had given him half a pint for his supper instead of the usual pint. He had hit her with a larding iron, knocking out a tooth. Mary Anne had run up to her room, but he had followed her striking her many times with a poker. Moses Hatto met his death in Aylesbury in mid-November.

1907 It was on this day in the tiny hamlet of Hoe Benham that two young artists, holidaying from London, were expecting a friend. Clarissa, a local artist, probably with more enthusiasm than talent, was about to arrive. One of the young men looking along the roadway saw Miss Clarissa Miles approaching, not only with her palette and easel but also chaperoned by a large, white, long-snouted pig. On her arrival she was questioned about her porcine companion but denied all knowledge. This was just another example of the many and varied animal ghosts that populated the area. The animals, always domesticated (such as pigs, sheep and goats), were thought to be owned by Tommy King who farmed locally; he was not popular and tended to be a recluse. In the late eighteenth century he hanged himself. His body was not discovered for some time and it is rumoured that some of his animals starved to death.

2 NOVEMBER

1945 In a Wokingham court a woman from Slough pleaded guilty to bigamy. It seems the lady would have succeeded in her deception had she not drawn the Army allowance in respect of her two husbands at the same post office. She was bailed to Reading Assizes but the final outcome is unknown.

3 NOVEMBER

1850 At Reading county sessions Harry Johnson was found guilty of poaching in the grounds of W.H. Hartley Esq at Bucklebury. He was fined £1 with one month of hard labour in default.

4 NOVEMBER

1850 David West was found guilty at Reading county sessions of pulling heath and stealing heather at Stratfield Mortimer, the property of R. Alfrey Esq. He was fined £1 2s 6d with one month of hard labour in default.

5 NOVEMBER

1850 On this day George Garret was brought before the magistrates at Reading county sessions charged with stealing two elm boards from Berry Farm, the property of Richard Fellows Esq of Bradfield. Two of Fellows's farm workers stated that they had seen the accused sawing and stacking elm boards at Berry Farm. Later in the evening they had met Garret carrying two boards on his shoulder. In the morning they found the pile was two boards short. Garret, who declined to make a statement, was sent for trial at the assizes. The magistrates decided that the case was far too serious to be dealt with at this level, so Garret was held in custody until the county sessions, where he received three months' imprisonment.

6 NOVEMBER

1890 At Newbury Police Court Anne Mary Dibley was charged with being drunk and disorderly. PC Holliday told the court that on the previous Saturday night he had come across the accused in a deplorable state. She had begged him to take her to the police station as her husband was looking for her and would beat her if he found her in this condition. The prisoner then collapsed and it

7 NOVEMBER

took him and PC Cook an hour to get her 200yds to the station. In her defence Anne Mary Dibley stated that she was not drunk but had had fits. She had wanted to go to the police station because there was nobody at home to look after her. She was fined 10s with seven days' imprisonment in default.

8 NOVEMBER 1830 The *Windsor Express* reported the 'Capture of a Resurrectionist', following the burial in Burnham churchyard of the wife of a poor man named Newell. Newell was suspicious that his wife's body might be exhumed and sold to surgeons, so for several nights he kept watch but nothing happened. However, on the Wednesday night he observed two men unearthing his wife's grave. He ran towards them; one instantly ran away but the second, a giant of a man, attacked him with a bludgeon. A violent battle ensued but Newell managed to disarm his attacker. The scuffle attracted the attention of some cottagers who lived nearby and together they overpowered the grave-robber and locked him in a cage. The next morning the prisoner was taken before magistrates at Beaconsfield, where, after examination, he was taken by constables to Aylesbury Gaol. 'When the constables were conveying the accused through the village the populace showered a plentiful supply of rotten eggs at him and it was with difficulty that they prevented them from doing him serious injury.' The *Express* went on to say: 'Newell has always borne the character of a very quiet well-behaved man and by his exploit on Wednesday night he has also proved himself strong and courageous.'

The capture of a resurrectionist in Burnham. *(Slough & Windsor Express)*

9 NOVEMBER 1830 On this day two men approached magistrates at Windsor asking if they should be rewarded for killing a mad dog. They were referred to the churchwardens, from whom they received a sum of money. The dog was killed on the previous Tuesday but not before it had bitten two other dogs which were still at large. Windsor's mayor had very properly ordered that all dogs should be tied up for the present.

10 NOVEMBER 1887 Frank Clayton, a boy of ten, was found guilty at Maidenhead of stealing 7½d, twelve steel pins and twelve rubber bands from Messrs Mills & Lynn. His brother, who accompanied him on this exploit, was not charged as he was only seven. Clayton was ordered to receive eight strokes with a birch rod and told that next time he could receive a custodial sentence.

11 NOVEMBER 1886 This was the day that Robert Whall, known locally as 'Drunken Bob', refused to do his allotted task of chopping wood at Cookham Union Workhouse. Whall was reported as saying: 'I ain't well.' At Maidenhead court, later in the month, a Dr Plumbe stated that he had examined Whall

on the premises; he was suffering from rheumatic pains but could do light work such as chopping wood. Whall was found guilty and fined fourteen days' hard labour.

1887 Maria Dyke of Woolhampton was found drunk in North Brook Street, Newbury. PC Keel, who arrested Dyke, stated that she had taken some goods from a shop and would neither pay for them nor go away. The shopkeeper had retrieved the goods and did not wish to press charges. In her defence Dyke stated that she had 'taken a little drink and did not know what had come over her'. She was fined 10s with seven days' imprisonment in default.

12 NOVEMBER

1867 Jane Watts was brought before Newbury Borough Court on this day charged with misbehaving during prayers at the Union Workhouse. Watts, a middle-aged pauper, was also accused of biting Arthur Henry Hale, an officer at that place. Hale stated that during prayers Jane Watts had pulled faces and put her body in various supposedly humorous poses. The visiting clergyman requested that Hale put her outside. This he proceeded to do, but owing to her great weight and her biting his hand he was obliged to drop her outside the door. Watts was found guilty and, because of previous convictions, she was sentenced to twenty-one days in Reading Gaol. Before leaving Watts shouted that 'twenty-one years wouldn't bother her'. 'Twenty-one days should suffice,'

13 NOVEMBER

North Brook Street,
Newbury, where
Maria Dyke of
Woolhampton had
'taken a little drink'.
(Newbury Library)

stated the mayor. Watts's parting gambit was that she much preferred Reading Gaol to the workhouse.

14 November   **1851** This day brought the death of Hannah Carey who, with her husband Jon, aged forty-seven, fifteen years her senior, kept the Leathern Bottle at Jealotts Hill near Warfield. She had been so badly beaten by her husband that she finally expired nearly two weeks after the incident. The Leathern Bottle was a small inn on the Bracknell to Maidenhead Road and did not make sufficient profit to keep Jon, Hannah and their two sons. Therefore John Carey also ran a small farm. This meant he had to be away all day while Hannah looked after the customers. This she did well, too well in one case, that of George Parker.

Parker was a recent widower. He was also young, attractive and needed a shoulder to cry on. It was a short step from Hannah's shoulder to her marital bed, a step that was regularly taken most afternoons. Jon Carey, however, was nobody's fool; he had noticed a change of attitude in his wife, her culinary skills and her sexual appetite were decidedly lacking. Carey knew that there was a man and he knew it to be George Parker. There were rows, with Hannah occasionally sporting a black eye. As time went on, however, she

The promiscuous Hannah Carey was finally laid to rest at Easthampstead church. *(Les Howard)*

became less surreptitious and more blatant. She flaunted her love affair in front of her husband and the customers.

Carey was reaching the end of his tether. One night he refused Parker a pint and told him to leave and never to return. Hannah, ignoring her husband, poured the pint and gave it to Parker, free of charge. Strangely enough Carey suffered this state of affairs for five years before he finally snapped. The affair culminated in a terrible bedroom scene, with Carey giving his wife a ferocious beating and then placing the bed on top of her and jumping up and down on it until his anger was spent. He then stayed all night holding the unconscious form of his much-loved Hannah. In the morning a Dr Thompson was fetched, as was Hannah's sister, Esther Bruton, and John Wigg the Warfield constable. Hannah died on 14 November and was laid to rest at Easthampstead Church, which was her dying request. Before Baron Platt at Reading Assizes in February 1852, Carey pleaded guilty to manslaughter. His fifteen-year-old son pleaded in his father's defence and stated that they were a happy family until Parker came on the scene. Jon Carey was sentenced to seven years' transportation; he begged not to be separated from his sons but Baron Platt would not be moved.

1784 The *Reading Mercury* reported that on this day the Bath coach came across a body lying somewhere near Southcote Lane. The corpse turned out to be that of Mr Wyatt, a wealthy sheep dealer from Englefield. The coach's guard was immediately despatched to Newbury while the coach continued on its journey to Reading. On returning with assistance, the guard was surprised to find the body had been carried some distance and most of the clothes stripped from it. The *Mercury* suggested that footpads had been disturbed by the Bath coach and had hidden themselves until it was safe to continue with their villainous task. The poor gentleman's purse was found some distance away minus £40. The thieves were never apprehended.

15 NOVEMBER

1830 A terrible murder took place this day at Mortimer West End, near Reading. Charlotte Billimore, an orphan child of eight years old, was returning from school with two friends. At the top of the hill they left her to continue home alone. She did not return that evening and the alarmed cottagers with whom she lived spent that night and the following two days looking for her. On Thursday a young man looking for a straying cow found the young girl's body in a wooded dell. It had been terribly mutilated. A description of the mutilations was provided at the Coroner's Court.

16 NOVEMBER

The head was down in the ditch with the body, which was bare, hanging down the inclination with the legs on the bank. Some of the skull bone was lying near the feet, as also were some of the brains. The right foot had been cut off and placed about two feet from the body. The body had been cut open from the throat to the lower belly and the entrails were lying on the bank; the eyes were hidden by the skin of the skull that had been peeled back. The right thigh was cut and the left leg broken.

A diabolical murder at Mortimer. A child's dismembered body was found here. (*Reading Mercury*)

A far more professional description was given by Dr William Wall, a Mortimer surgeon. The coroner then asked Dr Wall if he thought that the body had been dismembered by a person with surgical skills. He replied that parts of the skull must have been removed by forceps or pincers and that the work was precise and would have taken considerable time. An eccentric character named Robert Byles was brought before the jury. It was known that he was partly a recluse with considerable surgical skills. After many detailed questions Byles proved that at the time of the murder, 4.30 p.m., he was drinking 3 miles away at Lamberend.

DIABOLICAL MURDER NEAR READING.

On Monday week, a murder was committed at Mortimer West-end, about nine miles from Reading, which, for the cruelty used in perpetrating it, is almost without parallel. The facts of the case, as far as we have been able to learn, are these:—Charlotte Billimore, an orphan child, about eight years of age, (and who was under the protection of a person named Ford, residing in a cottage at a small distance from the spot), was on her return from school: she was in company with two other children till she arrived on a hill, where they left her to go home, and she was shortly after met by a woman, which was the last time she was seen alive. The cottagers whom she lived with became alarmed at her absence so long after school hours, and were out all that evening and the next day searching for her; but to no purpose, for they could not hear the least tidings of her. On Thursday, however, a young man, who was looking for a sow which had strayed away, went into a hedge-row, and in a pit there, filled with underwood and thick bushes, found the corpse of the child, mutilated in the most horrid manner it is possible to describe! The head was split open, and scalped; the body was cleft from the throat downwards, the bowels taken out, and laid on the ground; one leg was actually cut off, the thigh dislocated, and the other leg broken in two places!—presenting altogether a spectacle that makes the human frame shudder with horror. The pit is close to a field through which the child had to pass; and it is supposed that the fiendish wretch must have laid wait for his innocent victim, and seized her as she approached the fatal spot. That part of the parish where the murder was committed lies in Hampshire, so that the authorities had to send to Winchester for a coroner, Mr. Shebbeare, of Basingstoke, being from home.

Suspicion having fallen on a man named Miles, who has been absent from the village since the deed was perpetrated, many persons of the neighbourhood went in pursuit of him, and he has since been apprehended at Mattingly, a short distance from Mor-

He had several witnesses. The coroner's jury found that Charlotte Billimore had been murdered by persons unknown. An unprecedented £100 reward was offered 'for the arrest of this monster'.

17 November   **1558** On this day Elizabeth I was crowned Queen of England and Simon Alleyn, the vicar of Bray, changed his allegiance for the fourth time. During his time at Bray martyrs had been burned at Windsor and Thomas More, Chancellor of England, had perished. Realising that martyrdom was not for him, Alleyn had been twice a Catholic and twice a Protestant as religion changed sides with the monarchies of Henry VIII, Edward VI, Mary and finally Elizabeth I. When accused of being a turncoat an affronted Alleyn stated: 'Not at all, it is my destiny to remain the vicar of Bray.' A song, which can be traced back to the early eighteenth century, ends:

> And this is law, I will maintain
> Unto my dying day, Sir,
> That whatsoever King shall reign,
> I will be the Vicar of Bray, Sir!

18 November   **1830** This was the beginning of the machine riots at Newbury, when farm labourers broke machinery and destroyed buildings. The riot was quelled by a detachment of Grenadiers sent down from London.

19 November   **1787** Richard Dylon was committed to Reading Gaol by the mayor of Windsor for inhumanly biting the lip off one David Ireland. Ireland's life was in the most imminent danger, as he could not gain sufficient nourishment to sustain him.

1830 A mob at Hungerford smashed threshing machines then continued to Newtown where they met with the Inkpen gang and destroyed more equipment and set barns alight. Back at Hungerford several magistrates were surrounded by men with iron bars, hoes and cudgels who were demanding 12s a week. The terrified magistrates agreed. The mob then proceeded to Froxfield, where they stopped gigs and coaches in order to demand money.

1867 At Newbury William Bartle, landlord of the Greyhound Inn, was summoned for allowing prostitutes to assemble on his premises. PC Rosier stated that he had watched the inn from a neighbour's window. He saw six well-known girls of bad character. According to the *Reading Chronicle* PC Rosier then gave evidence too delicate to report. William Bartle was fined £2 by the mayor and warned about his licence.

1913 A noisy affray was erupting on this day in Reading's Basingstoke Road outside the Four Horseshoes public house, but drink did not seem to be an issue. There were many accounts of what happened but for brevity and clarity the case of Mrs Wix follows: Arthur Fennell, aged fourteen, of Grays Farm, Basingstoke Road, had been convicted of stealing tools from Manor Farm. The main witness had been Mrs Wix's seven-year-old son. At 11.15 a.m. on 22 November, Edward Fennell, the convicted boy's father, had hammered on her door and demanded to see her husband 'to sort it out'. Unfortunately Mr Wix was working away.

A terrified Mrs Wix shouted to a passing coalman, Ernest Hamm, to get PC Pocock. Hamm shot round the corner and then returned without calling

The Four Horseshoes, where a fatal affray took place. This was also where John Lancelot Martin (above), the well-known pathologist, examined the body of John Bridgewater. *(Berkshire County Library)*

the constable although he told Fennell that he had. His diplomacy got him into trouble. Fennell grabbed a stick and beat him across the head for several minutes. Hearing the disturbance two labourers, Bridgewater and Bolton, tried to restrain Fennell; Bridgewater was knocked to the ground and Bolton received two black eyes. Harry Childe, a decorator, tried to encircle the group with his motor car. Finally, he and several regulars from the inn managed to restrain Fennell, but not before he had delivered a kick to the prostrate Bridgewater.

On Monday 25 November John Bridgewater, aged forty, died of an infection at the Royal Berkshire Hospital. The following day Edward Fennell, described as a horse-dealer, was arrested for murder. On the following day John Lancelot Martin, the internationally known pathologist, had to decide whether or not Bridgewater had died through the direct action of Fennell.

Although it was proved that his demise was brought about by a germ picked up in hospital, the coroner's jury brought a verdict of wilful murder. The case, when it came to Reading Assizes on 17 January, had been reduced to manslaughter. In court Fennell admitted being angry when he came to Wix's door; he had heard that Wix had paid his son *2s 6d* to give evidence against his boy. When he saw Hamm, Bolton and Bridgewater, knowing them to be friends of Wix, he suspected a trap. The jury went out at 4 p.m. and returned after an hour bringing in a surprise verdict of not guilty, a popular decision with Fennell's many followers.

23 NOVEMBER **1940** On this day eight German bombs fell on Broadmoor: four on the estate caused little damage; a fifth landed harmlessly in a cottage garden; a sixth in the piggeries; the seventh fell into Somerset House causing a vast crater but no loss of life; and, finally, the eighth, which also landed in Somerset House and burst the water main, leaving the whole establishment without water. The supply, however, was returned within three hours. Clearly a prompt and efficient plumber attended. In those days plumbers earned £2 *10s* a week.

24 NOVEMBER **1658** Hungerford town authorities were worried at this time about the increasing price charged for flogging women. John Savage, the town beadle, had recently charged *2d* for publicly flogging Dorothy Miller.

25 NOVEMBER **1830** Reports were coming in at Faringdon of an 'incendiary', calling himself 'Swing', who had set fire to new labour-saving farm machinery and several barns, causing workers to be re-employed at ludicrous rates. Special constables were assigned to capture and detain any strangers seen at night.

26 NOVEMBER **1891** Thomas William Watts, a shop assistant, was charged with systematically robbing his employer, Mr Wakefield, of East Hagbourne. Watts was accused of stealing £114 *1s 7d* (an astronomical sum) over a year of employment. Wakefield, suspicious of Watts, sent several of his associates in to purchase goods. The assistant took the money but failed to register it or deposit it in the till. In the company of a constable, Wakefield went to Watts's

East Hagbourne, said to be Berkshire's prettiest village. In 1891 Thomas William Watts was charged with systematically robbing his employer of £114 1s 7d, a huge amount of money at the time. (*Berkshire County Library*)

bedroom and forced open his box. Under the assistant's clothes they discovered over £84. Back in court the mayor of Newbury decided that the case was far too serious to be dealt with locally and remanded Watts to Reading Assizes. Unfortunately the outcome is unreported. One can only assume that Watts was found guilty and, considering the vast amount of money involved, transported for many years.

1830 At Wallingford special constables were signed on to combat the many riots in the town. Marchers, intent on causing trouble, had destroyed machinery at outlying farms and had then surrounded the town. Local papers reported that the rioters were put to flight by the 'courageous and glorious constables'.

27 NOVEMBER

1866 Eliza Shaw, a Newbury prostitute, lived with and in fear of Henry Martin, who was in prison for robbery with violence at Thatcham; violence that Eliza had experienced regularly and was now glad to be without, albeit for only a few weeks.

28 NOVEMBER

While Martin was away Eliza started an affair with James Brett, a barman at the Eagle Tavern. It was on 28 November that Martin, released from prison earlier that day, confronted Eliza and Brett in the Eagle. Tempers flared and there was a brief struggle before the parties were separated and sent on their way. Later that night, after arming himself with several implements, Martin made for a house at Eyle's Buildings, the abode of James Brett – the cottage where Eliza and her new love lay in each other's arms.

Neighbours breaking into the cottage the following morning found Eliza dead and James Brett dying. Their wounds were horrendous. The murderer had attacked with a knife, hammer and butcher's hook. The following day found Henry Martin at the Crown Inn at West Mills on the banks of the Kennet and Avon Canal. After a couple of drinks he walked a short distance up the towpath to the footbridge at Northcroft. There he took off his neckerchief, tied it around his ankles and jumped into the icy water. His body was discovered later in the day.

29 NOVEMBER   **1865** This is reputed to be the last time that Aldermaston lock-up was used. The inmate was a drunk; his name is unknown. This is possibly incorrect, because rumour has it, though this was never confirmed, that 'Ban the Bomb' marchers in the 1960s broke in and spent the night there.

30 NOVEMBER   **1923** This was one of the nights when the Moonboy was seen at Tidmarsh. The apparition, which reserves itself for clear nights, is said to be that of a young boy drowned in a nearby stream. Two locals, returning from the Greyhound pub to their home near the rectory, saw the back of a young boy manifesting itself from the stream.

Luckily for the locals the spectre did not turn round, since homespun local legend dictates that if one sees the boy's face, terribly bloated by spending so long in the water, a death in one's close family is absolutely unavoidable.

The Aldermaston lock-up was last used on 29 November 1865. Its occupant was an unnamed drunkard. (*Brenda Allaway*)

DECEMBER

Chalvey, Slough, where Charles Dance had a small coal business. Dance was murdered on 22 December 1888. *(Berkshire County Library)*

1 DECEMBER **1893** This was the day that a young labourer named Chattin, at Cock-a-Dobby, Little Sandhurst, was refused a drink on credit at the Fox and Hounds. He promptly went outside and cut his throat with a razor. The young man was saved by a passer-by who administered first-aid. PC Goddard was soon on the scene, and he arranged for Chattin to be taken first to hospital and then to the cells at Sandhurst. Chattin was later charged and sentenced to seven days' hard labour, presumably as a deterrent to discourage him from attempting suicide on a regular basis.

2 DECEMBER **1830** At Wantage the farm riots were getting out of hand. A group of farm labourers waylaid servants and other workers, preventing them from going to work. Mobs also smashed farm machinery in Challow, Childrey and Sparsholt. A total of 200 rioters held farmers under siege in villages across north Berkshire. Mr Gibbs, a farmer from Lochringe, was lucky to escape with his life when he tried to prevent rioters burning his barn to the ground.

3 DECEMBER **1893** John Carter, said to be the most evil man in the county, was hanged on this day for killing his wife Rhoda. Carter, a blacksmith, lived with his third wife Rhoda at Watchfield, a small village near Wantage. He was known for his quick temper, as was Rhoda, who at thirty was seventeen years his junior. On 20 July, late at night, Thomas Carter, aged nine, heard an extremely violent row between his parents. In the morning he could not find his mother and was packed off to do various jobs with his younger brother before going to school.

When she arrived mid-morning, Mrs Titcombe found no sign of her daughter Rhoda. 'She has gone to see her sister at Eastleigh. She could be gone for a couple of days,' shouted John before slamming the door in her face. Mrs Titcombe found that strange, firstly because her daughter had not dropped in to see her (she only lived 50yds away), and secondly because she could see Rhoda's only decent green coat hanging in the hall.

Watchfield, where little has changed since the untimely deaths of three of John Carter's wives. *(Brenda Allaway)*

All that day the villagers of Watchfield coughed and spluttered as billowing, black, thick and sickly smelling smoke rose above Carter's smithy. Several people knocked on the door but were told to 'Go away', or words to that effect. Smoke was still billowing on 22 July when Dave Titcombe, Rhoda's brother, knocked on the door. Dave was suspicious but only told Carter he was worried the house would catch fire. Carter told his brother-in-law that he was boiling water for a shave and he was thinking of boiling some offal later. Titcombe, not satisfied with any of Carter's explanations, set off on a 30-mile round trip to Eastleigh to see if his sister was there. By this time Anne Butler, Rhoda's only friend, had set off to inform the police of her suspicions. At 1 p.m. PC Sparkes called at Carter's smithy but could not find him there. He returned an hour later, at 2 p.m., only to be told by Thomas that his father was out looking for Rhoda. That evening Sparkes was approached by a worried Dave Titcombe; he had been to Eastleigh but there was no sign of Rhoda.

PC Sparkes finally interviewed Carter on 23 July. Carter stated that he had searched everywhere and now believed that his wife had left him. The constable knew Carter to be lying but could do little to prove it. He made a quick search and then returned to the station. On 25 July John Carter told his brother in a Wantage pub that he had killed his wife. On 26 July, after wrestling with his conscience, Carter's brother reported the conversation to Wantage police. On 27 July Carter was arrested for the murder of his wife. While he was in custody police officers searched his smithy and found Rhoda's body only 3in under the dirt floor. The nose was smashed, the throat bruised and there had been an attempt to boil and burn the body. As Carter awaited his trial, local police began wondering about the strange disappearance of his second wife. According to Carter she had walked out on him, never to return. Dozens of officers from Faringdon and Wantage spent hours digging up an area known as Burnt Leas, but there was no sight of a body. On 16 November 1893 at Reading, Carter pleaded not guilty to murder. He claimed loss of temper and self-protection as Rhoda had been attacking him. The jury was not convinced and found him guilty. He was hanged at Reading shortly afterwards. Incidentally, Carter's first wife died in a very suspicious farm accident.

1882 At Maidenhead petty sessions Robert Whall ('Drunken Bob') faced his twenty-first charge of drunkenness. Whall apologised for his behaviour and begged not be sent to gaol, as there would be nobody to look after his wife and children. The mayor remarked that Whall was not doing a particularly good job of looking after them while he had his freedom. He was sentenced to twenty-one days' hard labour.

4 DECEMBER

1883 At Maidenhead petty sessions a young lad, Herbert Clover, was charged with cutting the skin of a drum owned by the Blue Ribbon Army. The assault on the instrument had occurred as the drum major attempted to lead the army on a march through town. The prosecution alleged that

5 DECEMBER

the damaged drum would cost 12*s* 6*d* to mend. Clover was fined 10*s* with 10*s* costs.

6 December **1916** On this day 'an elderly, well-dressed, bearded and half-balded man, of gentlemanly demeanour' was charged at Maidenhead with stealing a watch. The watch was hanging on a clip at the premises of Alfred Walzenker, a jeweller and watchmaker of Maidenhead. Later at Reading quarter sessions Dorothy Walzenker, elder daughter of the proprietor, stated that she had seen the accused put his hand through the open door and remove the watch from a clip at the back of the window. She chased him down the street and grabbed him around the knees. She then held him with the help of passers-by while her younger sister, Norah, went to fetch PC Parks. 'Does this man have the appearance of a common criminal?' asked the defence lawyer at the man's (Peter Quince's) trial. Possibly he didn't – but criminal he was. It emerged that Quince had served four terms of five years' imprisonment in the last twenty-five years under various aliases. Found guilty, he was sentenced to four years' penal servitude.

7 December **1793** Maidenhead Thicket was infested with highwaymen and footpads. Reputedly on this day Lord Bruce wrote to the Earl of Aylesbury, his father. The letter stated that a mutual friend, Lord Elgin, had had a fortunate escape from footpads who had attacked him. Lord Bruce went on to advise against travel across the Thicket, especially at night.

8 December **1933** On this day there were more reports of ghostly sighs coming from the Teardrop Room at the George Inn, Wallingford. The name referred to Room 3 where the plasterwork was painted with large tears or pears. The painting was said to have been made by an ex-landlord's daughter. Her prospective husband had been murdered and the girl, driven insane by grief, was confined

The George Inn at Wallingford where ghostly crying is heard from the Teardrop Room. (*David Beasley*)

to her room. There she had mixed soot and tears to make a mixture that she used as paint. The sighing sound has been heard quite regularly but the apparition is seldom seen. On the few occasions the forlorn lady has materialised, she is described as attractive but very, very sad. Most of the above is supposition, although there was a murder at the inn in 1626 and the perpetrator was hanged very close by.

1709 On this day, as on several other days, there were riots at Newbury. The riots started during an attempt to impress vagrants into the Queen's Service. A recent Act of Parliament had been passed stating that vagabonds and idle persons should be press-ganged into the Army or Navy.

9 DECEMBER

1770 Permission was granted on this day for several inns to be built in the forest near the village of Bracknell. The road from Ascot Heath to Reading was absolutely infested by highwaymen and it was thought that several inns would aid safety – though not that safe if one stopped at the Hind's Head (see 2 October).

10 DECEMBER

1876 The bodies of Inspector Joseph Drewitt and PC Thomas Shorter were discovered, less than 30yds apart, in Duncan Woods, near the village of Hungerford. Both men left widows and young children. The following day Newbury police revealed that Inspector Drewitt had been shot behind the ear and PC Shorter had been bludgeoned to death.

11 DECEMBER

By 9 a.m. the next day four local poachers were in custody: William Day (aged thirty-nine) and the Tidbury brothers, Henry (aged twenty-six), William (aged twenty-four) and Francis (aged seventeen). Witnesses had placed all four in the area of Duncan Woods. In addition a stick belonging to Henry Tidbury and a tobacco box, thought to belong to William Day, had been

The murdered PC Thomas Shorter and Inspector Joseph Drewitt. (*Berkshire County Library*)

PC William Golby found his colleagues' bodies. (*Berkshire County Library*)

The memorial at the fatal crossroads where Inspector Drewitt and Constable Shorter were murdered. (*Author's Collection*)

found. Footprints belonging to the younger two Tidbury brothers were later discovered.

When the assizes opened in mid-February the result seemed a foregone conclusion. There were a host of witnesses against the four men. Human blood had been found on their trousers, despite attempts to cover it up with red lead paint. From the witness box William Day stated that he had worked late and as he made his way home he came across William Tidbury leaning on a tree. There was a dark bundle on the ground. 'What's that?' he had inquired. 'Just a drunk,' came William Tidbury's reply. He then ushered Day out of the way and together they walked home.

Evidence pointing to Day's innocence came when PC Butcher reported a heated exchange between Day and William Tidbury while they were both incarcerated at Reading Gaol. Meeting briefly on the landing Day had shouted: 'I am not swinging for your crazy brothers, Bill. I wasn't there at the time and I'm damned if they're going to top me for your brothers. They're no bloody relatives of mine. If you want to, that's down to you, but I'm blowing the gaff. I'm not taking the bloody drop for them.' PC Butcher said that William Tidbury had tried to pacify Day, telling him everything would be all right.

Justice Lindley, in summing up, asked the jury if they believed that two strong police officers could be put to death and overcome by one man and a mere youth. Justice Lindley clearly did not think so and was fairly certain that all four men were involved. The crowd were very much of the judge's opinion. The jury, however, was not. They found William Day and William Tidbury not guilty of either murder and Henry and Francis Tidbury guilty of both murders. The court was stunned into silence.

Justice Lindley looked stern and dissatisfied. He reluctantly acquitted the two men and then, placing the black cap upon his head, sentenced the other two to death. Henry Tidbury admitted the crime from his cell and apologised to his brother Bill and William Day for involving them. Henry and Francis Tidbury met their maker on 12 March 1877. The *Reading Observer* described the event in great detail, even commenting on the bodies: 'The deceased looked livid and their necks appeared to be broken.'

12 December **1942** Below Basildon Park beside the River Thames a trio of Land Army girls reported a strange phenomenon. The Basildon House grotto was being used as the girls' hostel and the three described the appearance of the ghostly Lady Fane. True to form the silvery spectral lady appeared at 4.30 p.m. The ghost glided across the lawn and down to the river.

The Basildon House grotto on the Thames was where three Land Army girls witnessed the ghost of Lady Fane. *(Brenda Allaway)*

Lady Fane had lived in the grotto in the 1740s. There is said to be a bricked-up room and an underground passage from the grotto to the main house. How the lady died is also open to much speculation. Stories of her hiding in a self-locking chest have been overdone around the county; Marwell, Minster Lovell and Bramshill have been suggested as three of many such venues. The most likely story is the poor woman fell, jumped or was pushed into a deep well.

1976 This day brought a terrible accident at the famous Bear Hotel at Maidenhead. Anne Bailey, a serving girl, was burnt to death in the kitchen. It is thought that a stray spark flying from the range set her dress on fire. Mr Bennett, the proprietor, and his head waiter doused the poor girl with water and rolled her in a carpet, but to no avail. The Bear was no stranger to fire. In 1835 thirty-five mail and coach horses died when the stables caught fire. One horse, aptly named Miraculous, survived and worked for some years on the Bristol mail. The Bear along with the Greyhound were Maidenhead's two main inns. Travellers preferred to stay in town rather than face the notorious Thicket at night.

13 DECEMBER

1684 This is reputed to be the date that an overloaded ferry sank between Goring and Streatley. Reports stated that sixty lives were lost in the freezing water as drunken merrymakers returned from a ball. The accident caused a rift between the two villages for years.

14 DECEMBER

1830 The accidental death of coach driver Edward Jefferies happened on this day. Edward, an experienced coachman, met his death as the Stroudwater mail overturned near the Abingdon Turnpike on the Dorchester Road. At the

15 DECEMBER

post mortem John Casey, a bricklayer, stated that he had heard a frightening noise near his home at 2 a.m. Collecting his two sons he rushed out to see the mail overturned and one of the wheels across the head of the coachman. The guard, who was knocked unconscious, and a lady passenger who was trapped inside could say little as to the cause of the accident. A verdict of accidental death was recorded and the deplorable condition of the Abingdon roads was mentioned.

16 December   **1869**   On this day Rosa Rose set out with her two-week-old baby, Johnny, to walk to Warfield to see her mother. The distance was 12 miles and questions were to be asked later as to why Rosa had chosen to walk. Considering the distance, the filthy weather and the fact that she was not short of money it seemed strange indeed. The coach cost 5*d* and when Rosa and Johnny, soaked to the skin, rested at the Stag and Hounds, Binfield, Rosa had nearly £1 on her, nearly fifty times the price of the coach journey.

On 17 December Rosa knocked on the door of Mrs Emily Hearne at Church Street, Reading. Emily was a friend of Rosa's and had already helped her through an earlier illegitimate pregnancy. Emily stated that Rosa was drenched and she held the lifeless body of little Johnny in her arms. Mr Muggeridge, a surgeon who lived nearby, was called and after some examination he decided that the tiny baby had been immersed in water and had died under suspicious circumstances. The police were notified and Rosa was arrested and locked up at Reading police station.

After several remands Rosa Rose's hearing was heard within the walls of Reading Gaol on 23 January 1870. Rosa claimed that after taking liquid at the Stag and Hounds at Binfield she had carried on towards Warfield, a distance of less than 2 miles. On the way the heavens had opened and she had sheltered with Johnny in a shed. Overcome with exhaustion she had fallen asleep. She awoke at night to hear her baby boy crying outside the door. On examining Johnny she thought him to be dead. She panicked and stumbled into several water-filled ditches before finding the road and making her way back to Reading. The remainder of her story could be verified by Mrs Hearne and various other witnesses.

The inquiry decided that there was an indictment to answer and Rosa was kept in custody until the Lent Assizes. On 25 February the justices at the assizes ignored the indictment and Rosa Rose walked free without a word of evidence being heard. Reporters at the time were sceptical indeed. There were many questions that would not bear too deep a scrutiny.

17 December   **1873**   On this day the Marquess of Downshire, in a letter to *The Times*, expressed his concern and drew attention to the fact that of three criminal lunatics who had escaped from Broadmoor in the previous six months only one had been recaptured. In fact Lord Downshire's figures were at fault. Four inmates had escaped in 1873 and two had been recaptured. One of those who remained at large was a notoriously dangerous murderer named Bristow. He was never heard of again.

The Stag and Hounds, Binfield, where Rosa Rose stopped for refreshment with baby Johnny on the last day of his short life. *(Brenda Allaway)*

1867 This was a sad day for Wokingham. Henry Halliday, a very popular local family man, was thrown from his horse and cart near the Reading Road. Halliday died later in hospital and the newspapers reported that he would be greatly missed in the town.

1829 On this night in Abingdon John Moreton, 'a well-known turnip stealer', was stopped by a watchman and found to have in his possession a sack of turnips. The watchman, suspecting them to be the property of one John Munday, took Moreton back to Munday's farm, where he matched the stolen heads to the stalks. Moreton was committed to the assizes, but the outcome is unknown.

1884 On this day Jane Holt, an attractive widow, was at the end of her tether. She had been up most of the night worrying about Maria Shill. The night before she had taken two of Maria's young children Christmas shopping in town, leaving the youngest, a toddler, with Joseph Shill, Maria's husband.

Jane did not trust Joseph, as he was a toper and often violent when drunk. What Maria, thirty-two and attractive, saw in the hunchbacked draper she could not understand. Having returned with the two older children the previous evening and only receiving fuddled grunts from Shill, Jane had approached the police. PC Laney had gone to the property at 37 Victoria Cottages in Windsor and, on only hearing drunken snoring, had forced the window up some 10–12in and shone in his torch. The constable could see Shill snoozing on the bed with his youngest lying beside him. There was a bundle of clothes on the floor. One of the other children was pushed through the window to retrieve the toddler and Shill was left in sozzled peace.

The house where the Shills took a room was owned by George Grimsdale, Jane's son from a previous marriage. Jane also had an apartment on the premises. On that day Jane tried to persuade George to push the door in. George refused, saying that tenants were entitled to privacy, and anyway Joseph Shill had gone out earlier that morning. Mrs Prime, Maria's mother, had received a telegram on the same day. It came from Shill and stated that he believed Maria had committed suicide. In a state of fear and anxiety Mrs Prime and her two sons approached Grimsdale and asked to be let in, and once again the landlord refused. Joseph Shill returned on 21 December, slept deeply, then deposited his children with Jane Holt and left. In answer to Jane's worried questions he stated that he feared his wife had left him.

Shill had some unwanted and unwelcome visitors that day as he slurped a drunken pint at the Kings Head at Egham. The Prime brothers and Les Williams (who had once been betrothed to Maria) burst in and accused Shill of murder. Losing his temper Williams mercilessly beat Shill before being thrown out. Meanwhile Jane Holt had prevailed upon her son to open Shill's bedroom door. There, rolled in a blanket, was the blood-soaked corpse of Maria Shill. Her skull had been fractured half a dozen times with a flat-iron. Joseph Shill was arrested and charged with murder.

Before his trial at Berkshire Assizes evidence had been found that was damning; bloody trousers in the flat and blood-soaked shoes at Egham. The verdict was a foregone conclusion. The defence courageously alleged suicide, but Dr Norris, giving evidence, said that he had never heard of a case of anyone killing themselves by bashing their head with a flat-iron. Shill was found guilty of murder and hanged at Reading.

21 DECEMBER **1803** A reward of £5 was offered by Sheriff James Pither of Shinfield Road, Reading, for information leading to the apprehension of one Timothy Lee, who had deserted the Army and had previously worked as a labourer in Reading. He was thirty-eight, dark and 5ft 3in tall. He had previously avoided capture by disguising himself as a woman.

22 DECEMBER **1888** This was the night of the heinous murder of Charles Dance, a coal merchant of Chalvey. Dance's face had been smashed, his skull fractured and his bag, containing a substantial amount of money, was missing. Shortly afterwards, a local layabout, William James, was arrested. At his trial at least fifteen salient points were stated by the prosecution. Each substantiated and pointed to James's guilt; not the least of which were blood on his shoes and trousers, threatening his landlady to provide an alibi, borrowing 2*d* from a friend to buy beer at 6 p.m. and then spending lavishly at 8 p.m.

The landlord of the Flags public house deposed that James had spent a fortune on drink for a local prostitute known as 'Whoops my Darlin'. James had accounted for his new-found fortune by saying he had drawn his Christmas money from the White Hart. This was denied by the landlord who claimed that James had defaulted in April. A man answering his description was also seen ascending a wall at Dance's coal yard. The prosecution felt sure that they had their man 'banged to rights'.

What the prosecution hadn't gambled on was the brilliance of a defence lawyer named Attenborough, and a most unexpected felicitous deposition from the Stanleys. James and Ann Stanley suddenly appeared to testify that William James had been at their home that night with some stolen chickens (hence the blood), and had stayed there during the time of the murder. William James was acquitted – a very lucky man indeed.

23 DECEMBER

1917   Pro-German, Belgian Louis Claas escaped from Reading Gaol on this day. Claas was an internee being held for the duration of the First World War. In 1918, after the Armistice, Claas returned to the gaol to visit old friends. He had been fighting in the 13th Battalion of the Middlesex Regiment. He was not permitted to enter.

24 DECEMBER

1874   Christmas Eve is not a good day to travel by train. Martha Pearce, a Wallingford witch, warned passengers of a disaster on that day. They took no notice. The train crashed at Hampton Gray with thirty-one fatalities. Also on Christmas Eve, in 1841, a London goods train pulled out of Twyford with seventeen goods trucks, two open trucks and thirty-eight passengers. Rain caused a terrible landslide; eight passengers were killed and fifteen seriously injured. Local papers reported 'a dreadful mutilation of dead bodies'.

25 DECEMBER

1886   Christmas Day brought the death of John Chapman, a lowly coachman working in Clewer, near Windsor. John's only claim to fame was that he was married to and then separated from Eliza Ann Smith. Eliza Ann (Annie) Chapman was short, stout and an alcoholic who turned to prostitution when John kicked her out after the death of their elder daughter. Annie was found murdered at 29 Hanbury Street, London, on 8 September 1888. She was the second victim of 'Jack the Ripper'.

26 DECEMBER

1794   A report in Wokingham states that Elizabeth North was buried on 26 December 1794. She was found dead, terribly bruised, the morning after a bullbaiting. The coroner at the inquest found her 'accidentally dead'. There was a side note: 'A man taken from the Bull is without hope of life.' In 1661 George Staverton, a businessman of Wokingham, bequeathed £6 per annum to provide a bull to be baited yearly. Massive crowds invaded the town on St Thomas's Day (21 December). The Wokingham fighters threatened, beat, robbed and bullied. Several people died either by accident or design; more than a few unwanted spouses were shoved under the oncoming crowds as they chased the bull through the narrow streets. The 'jollities' ceased when bullbaiting was outlawed in 1823.

27 DECEMBER

1868   On this day the *Berkshire Chronicle* reported that a Broadmoor inmate, Daniel MacLean, scaled the lower wall on Christmas Eve. MacLean was never recaptured.

John Chapman died on Christmas Day 1886 at Windsor. His claim to fame was that he was married to Annie Chapman, the second victim of 'Jack the Ripper'. *(Illustrated Police News)*

28 December **1808** After lying between life and death for nearly a week Martha May died on this day at Wokingham. Martha had been terribly injured by the Wokingham fighters during bullbaiting on St Thomas's Day.

29 December **1938** At the Berkshire Assizes Henry Carter, a one-legged ex-professional boxer, was found guilty of committing grievous bodily harm, but insane. Carter had been charged with attempted manslaughter when he attacked a

Bullbaiting at Wokingham on St Thomas's Day. Several people were killed at the event until it was declared unlawful in 1823. *(Berkshire County Library)*

MURDER OF A CHILD BY ITS FATHER.

A cold-blooded murder has just been perpetrated in the borough of Windsor. A coroner's inquest was held in the Council Chamber at the Town-hall, before Mr. Martin, on Tuesday, and at the same time the prisoner was brought before Mr. Holderness, the mayor, and two justices, when the evidence of several witnesses was to the following effect:—The prisoner, John Gould, residing at Clarence Clump, in the borough, the father of two children, had been in the habit of treating one of them, a fine little girl of between six and seven years of age, with great cruelty, and the poor child always went in fear of her inhuman parent. The mother of the child, being engaged at the Windsor Infirmary and Dispensary, had left the two children in care of a neighbour, and the father, who had been drinking for a whole week, returned home to dinner about three o'clock in the afternoon of Monday last, and the child had previously gone into the house to light the fire with some other children, and when the prisoner entered the house he turned all out excepting the unfortunate child. Shortly afterwards the prisoner went to a neighbour's house and said, "Mrs. Clarke, I want you." She followed him home, and when she got into the room she saw the floor covered with blood; the child on its knees with its hands on the step, and its throat cut. The prisoner stood with a razor in his hand, and said, "I have done it! I have done it!" He afterwards threw the child out of doors, when it was picked up by the neighbours, and conveyed to the dispensary, but it died before it reached there. The evidence of Mr. Ellison, surgeon, showed that the throat of the child had been cut about five inches in length, and that the jugular vein on the right side had been divided. Superintendent Eagar said the prisoner afterwards told him that he went home to get some dinner, and the child annoyed him by crying, and that he had done the deed through drink, and was now sorry for it. The prisoner, although drunk, was not so far gone as not to know what he was about.

He was committed to Reading gaol to take his trial for wilful murder. He is about 35 years of age.

neighbour. Lavinia May Chaplin stated that she lived near Carter at Chavey Down, near Ascot. He had been forced out of his house and lived in a tent in the woods. She provided him with food and the odd glass of beer when he called in at the Royal Foresters where she worked as a barmaid. Carter's response to such kindness was to call at her house and strike her over the head with a hammer.

1861 At 3 p.m. Samuel Wilkins, a twelve-year-old schoolboy, was passing Clarence Clump at Clewer, near Windsor. He stopped in his tracks at a terrible sight. Hannah Gould, aged seven, was bleeding profusely from a neck wound. Her father, John Gould, was shaking her and shouting: 'Won't clear up, won't you. You untidy little bugger.' Suddenly Gould

30 December

The whole county was shocked by the murder of Hannah Gould at Windsor. The tiny girl's throat had been cut by her hot-tempered father. *(Reading Mercury)*

stood back horror-struck, dropped the tiny body to the floor and rushed to a neighbour's door. Fetching the neighbour, Sarah Clark, back to his house he stated, 'My God, my God, what have I done?' Meanwhile the schoolboy, Samuel Wilkins, was bravely trying to stem the flow of blood but to no avail; little Hannah Gould was dead. Five minutes later Wilkins had summoned PC Redbourn and after a ferocious struggle he and Charles Cockel, a neighbour, managed to handcuff Gould. At 4.30 p.m. John Gould was charged with the murder of his daughter. During his stay in Reading Gaol, Gould wrote a letter of confession. Found guilty at the assizes he was hanged on Friday 14 March 1862. Newspaper reports stated: 'Gould prayed for about five minutes but did not address the hostile crowd.'

31 DECEMBER **1916** New Year's Eve 1916 brought a report on the ghost of Eliza Kleininger at the Berystede Hotel at Sunninghill. In 1886, when the building was a private house owned by the Standish family, Eliza had been a French lady's maid there. On 27 October of that year a fire broke out, rapidly consuming the whole building. Eliza's charred bones were found near the badly burnt staircase. Around her were scattered the jewels and trinkets she had collected over her many years of service; it was thought that she had run into the building to collect them. When the building was reconstructed as a hotel one could be forgiven for thinking that Eliza might have returned on 27 October. But no, her spirit returns on New Year's Eve, when spirits are plentiful in all senses of the word.

The Berystede Hotel where the ghost of Eliza Kleininger was sighted on New Year's Eve 1916. Eliza had died in a fire there trying to save her trinkets many years before. (*Trusthouse Hotels*)

BIBLIOGRAPHY

Barham, Tony, *Thames Valley Witchcraft*, Bourne End, Spurbooks, 1973
Beckinsale, R.P., *Companion into Berkshire*, London, Methuen, 1951
McLoughlin, Ian, *Berkshire Murders*, Newbury, Countryside Books, 1992
Mee, Arthur, *Berkshire*, London, Hodder & Stoughton, 1939
Middleton, Tom, *Royal Berks*, Buckingham, Barracuda Books, 1979
Prescott, Martin, *Crow on the Thorn*, Martin Prescott & Associates, 1973
Watson, Michael, *Curiosities of Berkshire*, Seaford, S.B. Publications, 1996
Wilde, Oscar, *Ballad of Reading Gaol*, first published in 1898
Winchester, Simon, *Surgeon of Crowthorne*, Viking, 1998

Various editions of the following newspapers have been used:

Berkshire, Buckinghamshire
    & Surrey Advertiser
Berkshire Chronicle
Bracknell News
Camberley News
Henley Standard
Illustrated London News
Maidenhead Advertiser
Newbury Chronicle
Newbury Weekly News

Newbury Observer
Oxford Gazette
Reading Mercury
Reading Observer
Reading Standard
Slough & Windsor Express
Slough & Windsor Observer
Windsor Gazette
Windsor Herald
Wokingham Times

ACKNOWLEDGEMENTS

Thanks are due to Brenda Allaway for her photographs, David Beasley, Dave Blackman his for typing skills, Peter Bourne, the British Museum, Stewart P. Evans, Les Howard for the loan of his photographs, Angus McNaughton, Jeff Nichols, Tony Rance for helping to compile the text, Arthur Spicer, Michael Stiles, Bob Wyatt – and many, many more.

Special thanks must go to Berkshire County Library for supplying many of the photographs in this book and for the cooperation of the libraries at Newbury, Wokingham, Bracknell, Henley, Camberley, Maidenhead, Windsor and Slough.